MW00817129

Mel Bay's

Deluxe Encyclopedia of Guitar Chord Progressions

by Johnny Rector

The primary purpose of this advanced study is to give the guitarist the necessary fundamentals in chord progressions, extensions, alterations, substitutions, etc., so that he or she will acquire the knowledge essential to develop and create one's own ideas in chordal playing.

Order of Contents

Part — 1

Basic chord progressions and extensions. Popular chord progressions and extensions. Chromatic diminished 7th progressions. II7 to V7 chord progressions. The III (passing) chord. Chromatic minor 7th progressions. Chord progression application utilizing chords and progressions other than those found in basic, etc.

Part — 2

Dominant 7th substitute chord progressions. II7 to dominant substitute chord progressions. Altered dominant, and dominant substitute chord progressions. Fill-in progressions, substitutions. Utilization and application of chord study to standard progressions.

CD CONTENTS

1	Introduction and Tune Up [1:19]	21	Pg. 31 Examples [1:16]	41	Pg. 60 Examples [1:00]
2	Pg. 7 & Pg. 8 Examples [3:30]	22	Pg. 33 Examples [1:05]	42	Pg. 61 Examples [1:00]
3	Pg. 9 Examples [1:31]	23	Pg. 34 Examples [1:06]	43	Pg. 62 Examples [:59]
4	Pg. 10 Examples [1:32]	24	Pg. 35 Examples [1:23]	44	Pg. 63 Examples [:59]
5	Pg. 12 Examples [1:24]	25	Pg. 37 Review [:43]	45	Pg. 64 Examples [1:00]
6	Pg. 13 Examples [1:24]	26	Pg. 38 Review [:37]	46	Pg. 65 Examples [1:08]
7	Pg. 14 Examples [1:20]	27	Pg. 39 Examples [1:24]	47	Pg. 66 Examples [:49]
8	Pg. 15 Examples [1:09]	28	Pg. 40 Examples [1:10]	48	Pg. 67 Examples [1:13]
9	Pg. 16 Examples [1:29]	29	Pg. 42 Progression [:56]	49	Pg. 68 Examples [1:05]
10	Pg. 17 Examples [1:17]	30	Pg. 43 The III Chord [1:24]	50	Pg. 69 Examples [:58]
11	Pg. 18 Exmaples [1:09]	31	Pg. 44 Examples [1:02]	51	Pg. 70 Examples [:56]
12	Pg. 20 Examples [1:06]	32	Pg. 46 Chromatic Min. 7th Chords [1:17]	52	Pg. 71 Examples [:43]
13	Pg. 21 Examples [1:07]	33	Pg. 47 Examples [1:02]	53	Pg. 72 Examples [:38]
14	Pg. 22 Examples [1:07]	34	Pg. 49 & Pg. 50 Examples [1:29]	54	Pg. 73 Examples [1:45]
15	Pg. 24 Examples [1:05]	35	Pg. 51 Review [1:10]	55	Pg. 75 Examples [:45]
16	Pg. 25 Examples [1:25]	36	Pg. 52 [1:47]	56	Pg. 76 Examples [1:17]
17	Pg. 26 Examples [1:14]	37	Pg. 54 [1:31]	57	Pg. 77 Examples [1:35]
18	Pg. 28 Examples [1:06]	38	Pg. 56 [1:31]	58	Pg. 79 Examples [1:04]
19	Pg. 29 Examples [1:06]	39	Pg. 58 [1:22]	59	Pg. 80 Examples [:59]
20	Pg. 30 Examples [1:17]	40	Pg. 59 Examples [1:26]	60	Pg. 81 Examples [1:04]

Visit us on the Web at http://www.melbay.com — E-mail us at email@melbay.com

Johnny Rector, was born in Hickory, North Carolina. Started playing guitar at the age of 13. He has been a free-lance guitarist/ teacher in the Chicagoland area for the past 25 years. Studied guitar under Joseph DePiano of Chicago. Studied dance band arranging under the well-known Bill Russo of Chicago. Studied a condensed Joseph Schillinger method under Daniel Garamoni also of Chicago.

He is the author of several other well-known guitar books which have gained prominence throughout the country.

Johnny Rector is perhaps one of the most prolific writers of guitar material currently on the scene.

Playing chord progressions is vital to the guitarist of today. The demands of modern music make it necessary for the serious guitarist to study all aspects of the harmonic framework of his instrument. Johnny Rector is one of todays fine writers for guitar. It is my feeling that this text will be a thorough and valuable asset to the serious guitarist looking for indepth harmonic study on his instrument. I highly recommend this book for any guitar player regardless of style.

Foreword

Here, for the first time, is a treatise of modern CHORD PROGRESSIONS — EXTENSIONS — ALTERATIONS — SUBSTITUTIONS and APPLICATION. This extraordinary work is offered to meet the need of every guitarist—student, amateur, teacher, and professional.

The trend in modern music has made it necessary to replace outmoded books, that no longer suffice as vehicles to bring the guitarist, to the point of efficient performance demanded by constantly-evolving conceptions. This is the purpose of this study—it's exciting—it's an adventure never before encountered. This new approach is formulated to draw into focus a well-rounded degree of musical necessities for modern chordal playing.

This study is the first of its kind to be written for Guitar. It was written as a self-study for the guitarist who has not had the opportunity to study material of this kind with a first-class competent teacher-artist. This study will show unusual forms; progressions other than basic, etc. It will help you to develop a sensitive ear by establishing different chordal tonalities... this is a must for those who wish to be able to extemporize chordal progressions in the modern idiom.

Author's Note

This advanced study is divided into two parts. Part 1—"POPULAR PROGRESSIONS," with extensions, and Part 2—"MODERN PROGRESSIONS," with extensions, alterations, substitutions, and application. Part 1, contains the necessary explanations and exercises to conceive and understand popular chord progressions. Part 2, contains the more advanced chordal progressions.

It is the author's intention to explain this technic of chordal application in order to instruct those musicians who have not had the opportunity to acquire such knowledge because it had not been outlined for study prior to the publication of this treatise. Not only will the professional guitarist find the material interesting and exciting, but of tremendous value, as well.

The most common chord progressions are given, using the BASIC chords as a guide in all chord progression exercises, with examples of extensions, alterations, substitutions, etc. This is of PRIME IMPORTANCE, because when chords other than BASIC are used in the examples, it will show how these chords can be extended, altered, substituted under each type of chord— Major, Minor, Dominant, etc. Thru proper application, these chord progressions with extensions, alterations, etc., can be used in any song using the same basic progression or a combination of progressions. You may also use any passing chords, alterations, substitutions shown in the examples other than those given in the BASIC. Analyze and study each progression carefully. The main idea is to use chords other than BASIC, thru chord extensions, alterations, substitutions of chords, and to create a good bass and treble-line pattern, harmonically following the lead, or melodic line, in your accompaniment, or rhythm: This is called chord-voicing. This study is not a chord-solo style of playing, but it can be put to good use thru proper utilization and application.

Although this treatise was written as a self-study for the intermediate, advanced and professional guitarist, it is recommended for best results, that it be under the guidance of a first-class competent teacher-artist, understanding modern chordal progressions and its application. Part 1 should be studied thoroughly before attempting the study of Part 2.

JOHNNY RECTOR

Illustrations And Remarks

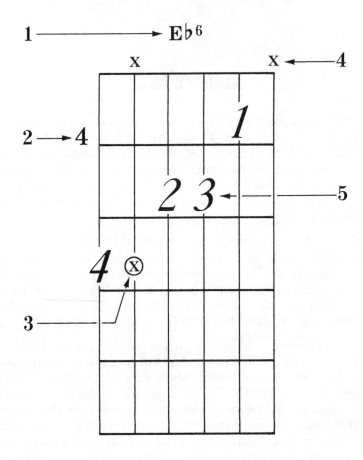

1. CHORD SYMBOL NAME.

2. NUMBER TO LEFT OF CHART INDI-
   CATES FRET AT WHICH CHORD STARTS.

3. (X) INDICATES OPTIONAL USAGE.

4. SYMBOL "X" INDICATES STRING WILL
   NOT BE SOUNDED OR PLAYED.

5. NUMBERS IN CHART INDICATE FIN-
   GERS USED FOR CHORD.

Here are four (4) different rhythms of many that may be played for any examples given in each chord progression exercise.

Release finger pressure after each stroke of chord for a crisp beat.

Play the bass note on the one count and the upper chord part on the two count. Same applies to count 3 & 4.

Hold the chord while playing first, and second count, releasing finger pressure indicated by rest.

Play the chords on the count of one and three, sustaining the chords as indicated. This rhythmic pattern is mostly used in jazz style playing.

In the illustration below, we use the chord progression exercise and examples on the following page to show the possible combinations for the I (C) to IV (F) and to V7 (G7) chord. You will note there are 16 possible combinations for any two chords. Using this procedure, many combinations are possible in each chord progression exercise. Each chord progression exercise and its examples throughout this study are to be practiced as shown below.

I MAJOR TYPE CHORDS	IV MAJOR TYPE CHORDS	V7 DOMINANT TYPE CHORDS
C6 — F6, Fma. 7, Fma. 9, F6/9	F6 — G7, G9, G7/6, G13	G7 (to any Major (I type chord
Cma. 7 — F6, Fma. 7, Fma. 9, F6/9	Fma. 7 — G7, G9, G7/6, G13	G9 (to any Major (I type chord
Cma. 9 — F6, Fma. 7, Fma. 9, F6/9	Fma. 9 — G7, G9, G7/6, G13	G7/6 (to any Major (I type chord
C6/9 — F6, Fma. 7, Fma. 9, F6/9	F6/9 — G7, G9, G7/6, G13	G13 (to any Major (I type chord

Any conceivable combination of chords in the above examples is possible.

7

Chord Progression - C, F, G7

Familiarize yourself thoroughly with all chords in charts before attempting to play any of the examples in exercise below. Chords given are of the most popular ones.

In Ex. 1, memorize and master the chord progression thoroughly.
Optional bass note is given in parenthesis.

Once you have mastered and can play from memory the chord progression in Ex.1, move up one fret to the key of Db. Play the same progression in the key of Db, (Db, Gb, Ab7) using the same formations as in the original key. When thoroughly familiar with the progression and formations in new key, move up another fret to the key of D, and proceed in the same manner as before. Continue through the key of G.

In Ex. 2, memorize and master this example in the same manner as Ex.1, and proceed with the principles set forth in Example 1, moving up one fret each time through the key of G. Same principles apply to Ex. 3 and Ex. 4.

Chord progression examples are presented in the order they follow under each type of chord for practical purposes as well as for simplicity in writing, and does not necessarily signify they follow in the order found best. See illustration page 7, and apply all possible combinations for best results. Continue this procedure to all examples of chord progression exercises in this study.

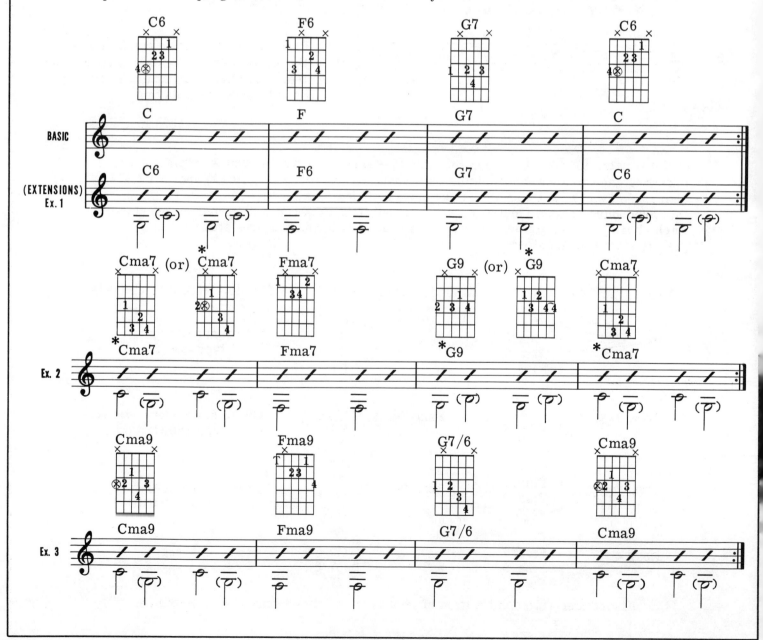

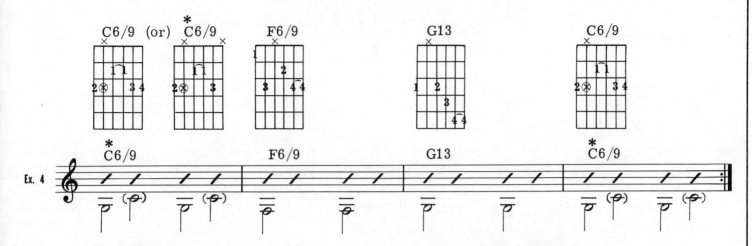

* Optional

For the ambitious guitarist; also play examples as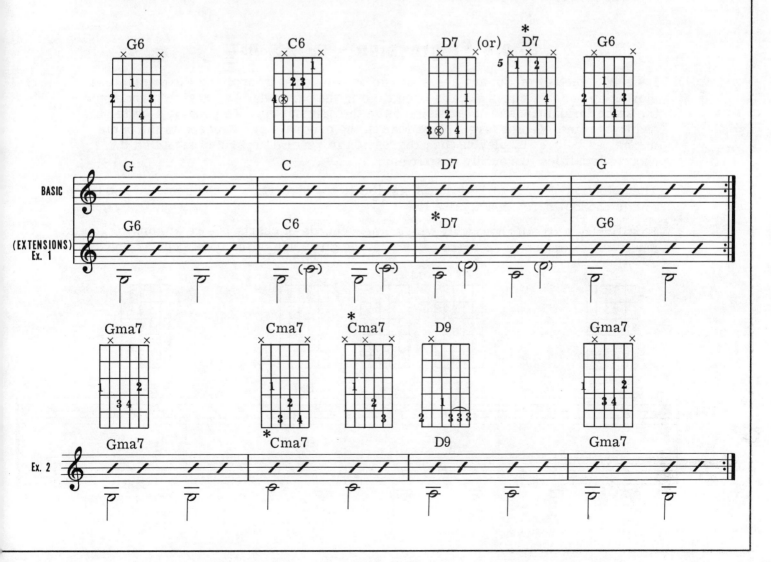

Any conceivable combination of chords in the above examples is possible.

Chord Progression - G, C, D7

Memorize and master throughly each chord progression example in the same procedure as before, and move up one fret chromatically each time to new key applying the same formations and progressions as in original. Continue thru the key of C.

The selection of tunes and/or songs is left to the discretion of the guitarist and teacher for chord progression application.

Familiarize yourself thoroughly with all new chords in charts before attempting to play any of the examples in exercise below. Chords given are of the most popular ones.

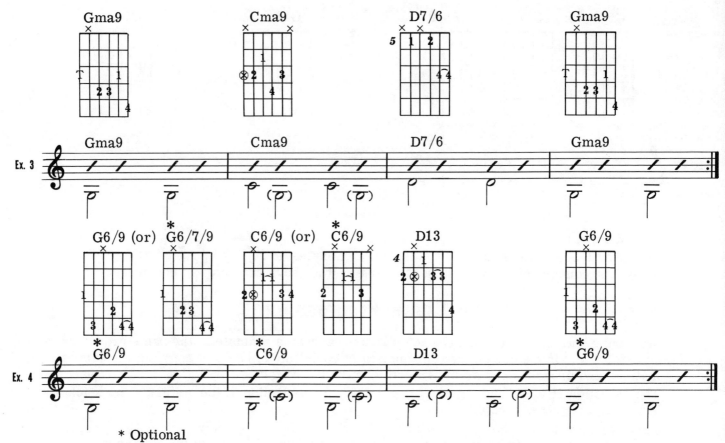

* Optional

Any conceivable combination of chords in the above examples is possible.

Chord Progression - E♭, A♭, B♭7

Let's take the key of E♭, and see what can be developed by applying the principle of moving up one fret chromatically each time to the particular key desired, and apply the same formations and progression as in the original key. To provide a better bass and treble line, we use forms other than in the original key. Proceed in the same manner as before, by playing the progression in several keys, and establish the chordal tonalities thoroughly in your ear.

The selection of tunes and/or songs is left to the discretion of the guitarist and teacher for chord progression application.

Familiarize yourself thoroughly with all new chords in charts before attempting to play any of the examples in exercise below. Chords given are of the most popular ones.

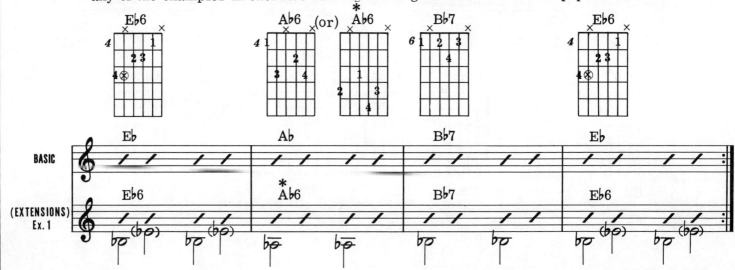

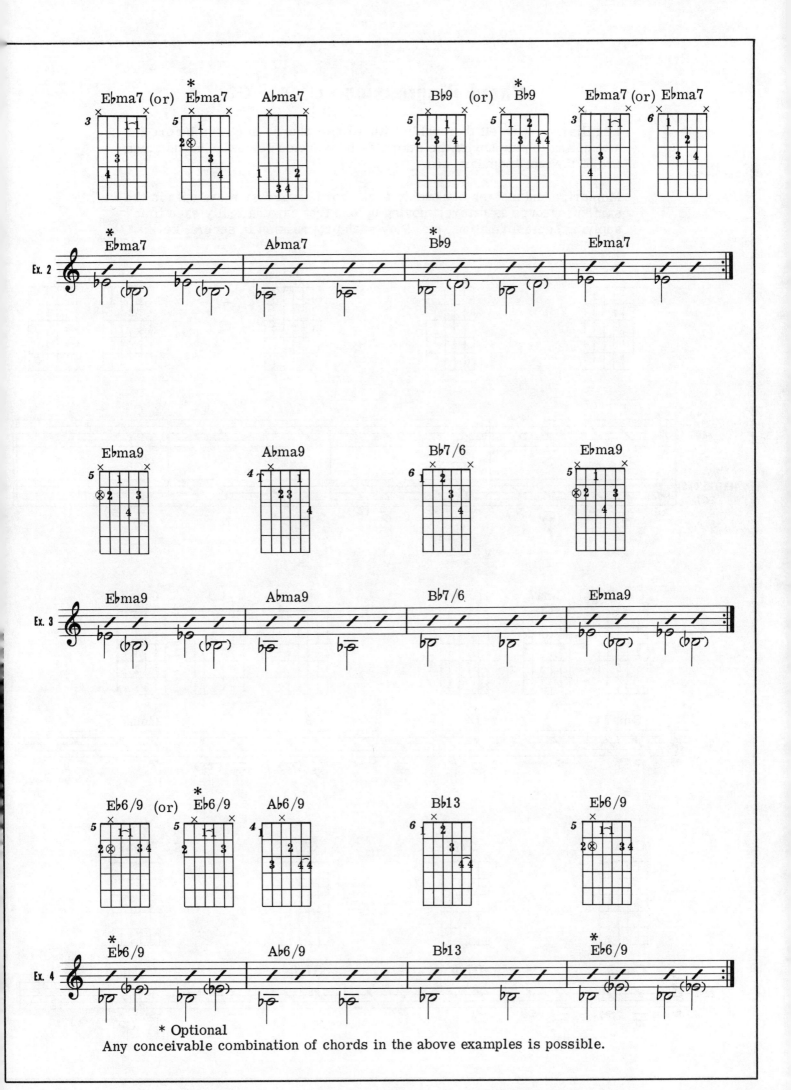

* Optional
Any conceivable combination of chords in the above examples is possible.

Chord Progression - C, D7, G7

Familiarize yourself thoroughly with all new chords in charts before attempting to play any of the examples in exercise below. Chords given are of the most popular ones.

Memorize and master thoroughly each chord progression example in the same procedure as before, moving up one fret chromatically each time applying same formation, etc. Play each progression in several keys.

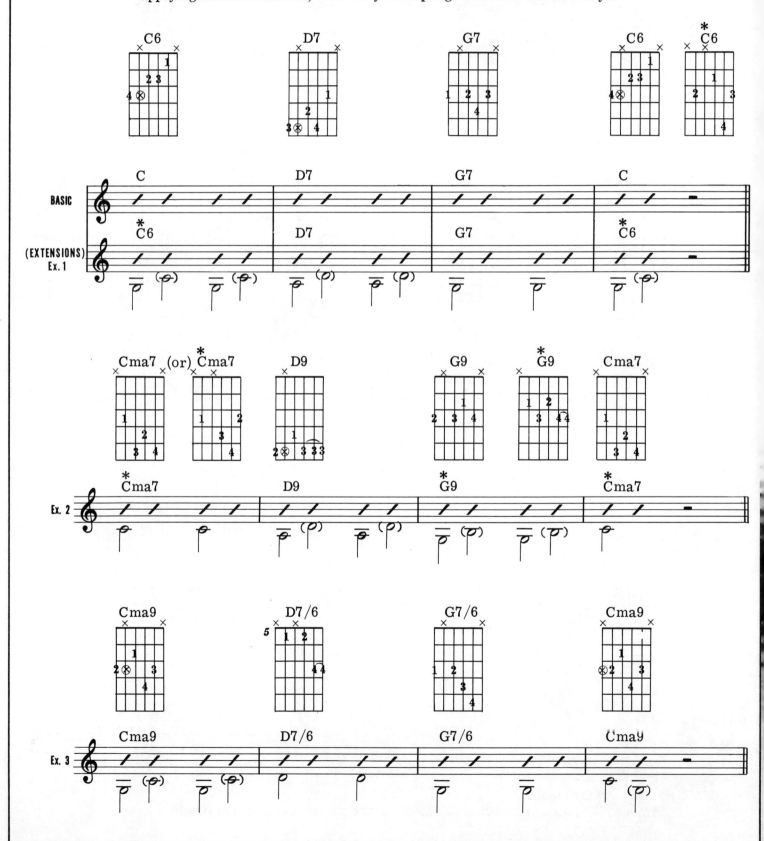

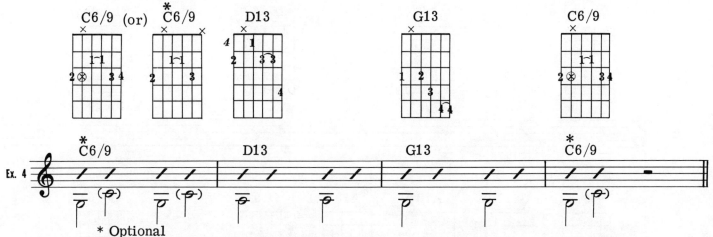

* Optional

Any conceivable combination of chords in the above examples is possible.

Chord Progression - G, A7, D7

Familiarize yourself thoroughly with all new chords in charts before attempting to play any of the examples in exercise below. Chords given are of the most popular ones.

Memorize and master thoroughly each chord progression example in the same procedure as before, moving up one fret chromatically each time applying same formation, etc. Play each progression in several keys.

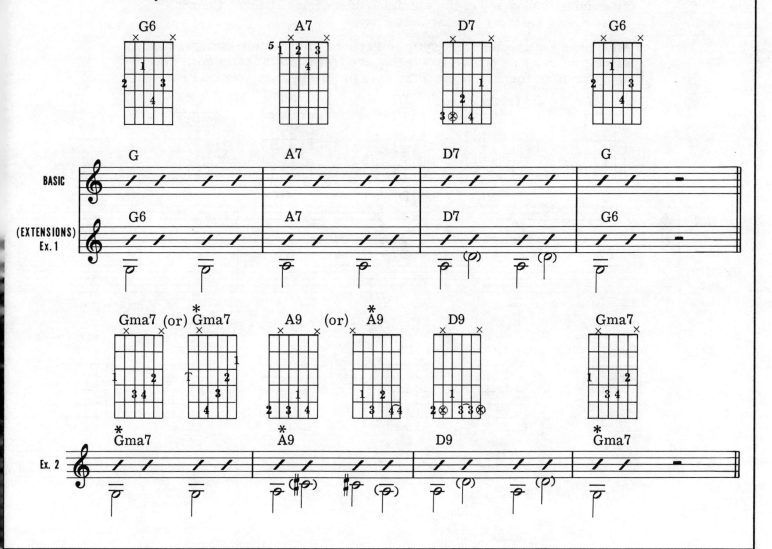

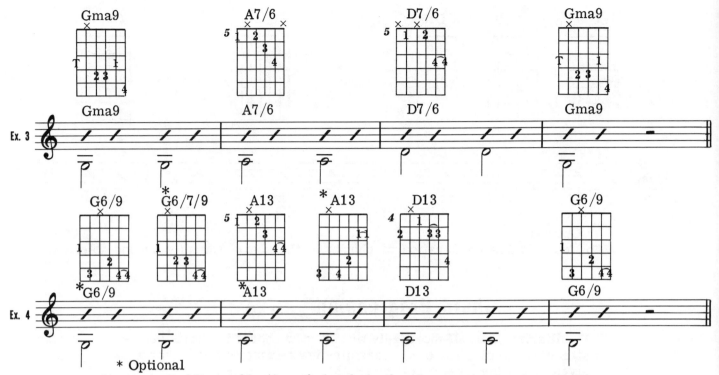

* Optional

Any conceivable combination of chords in the above examples is possible.

Chord Progression - C, A7, D7, G7

Familiarize yourself thoroughly with all new chords in charts before attempting to play any of the examples in exercise below. Chords given are of the most popular ones.

Memorize and master thoroughly each chord progression example in the same procedure as before, moving up one fret chromatically each time applying same formation, etc. Play each progression in several keys.

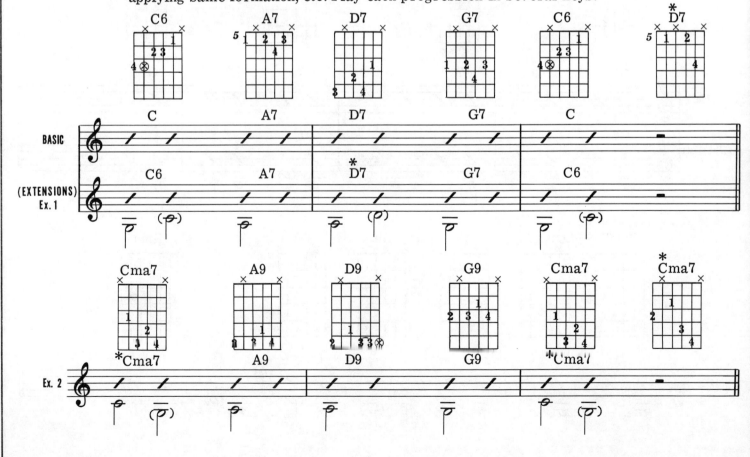

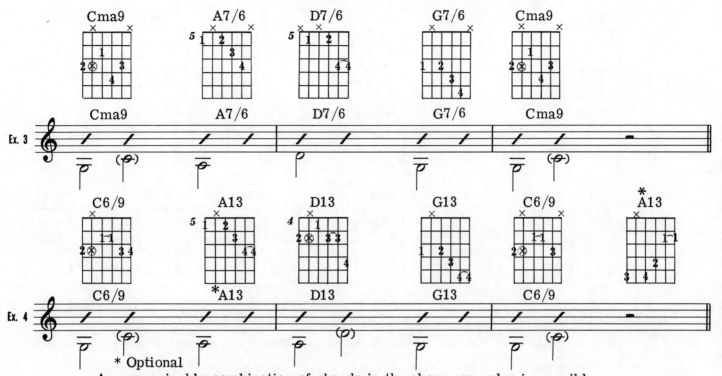

Any conceivable combination of chords in the above examples is possible.

Chord Progression - G, E7, A7, D7

Familiarize yourself thoroughly with all new chords in charts before attempting to play any of the examples in exercise below. Chords given are of the most popular ones.

Memorize and master thoroughly each chord progression example in the same procedure as before, moving up one fret chromatically each time applying same formation, etc. Play each progression in several keys.

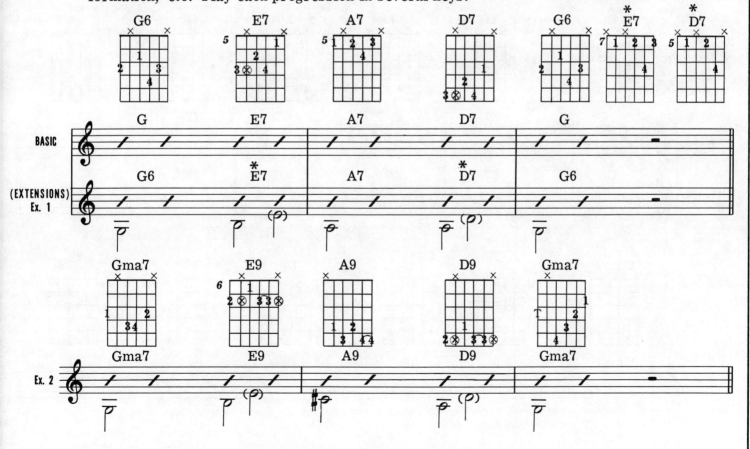

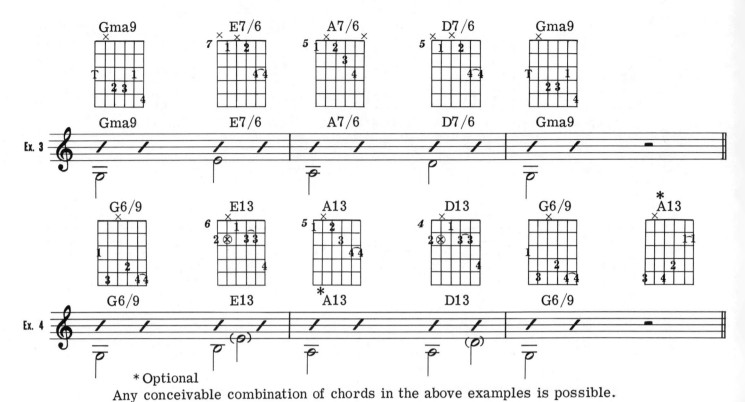

*Optional

Any conceivable combination of chords in the above examples is possible.

Chord Progression - C, E7, A7, D7, G7

Familiarize yourself thoroughly with all new chords in charts before attempting to play any of the examples in exercise below. Chords given are of the most popular ones.

Memorize and master thoroughly each chord progression example in the same procedure as before, moving up one fret chromatically each time applying same formation, etc. Play each progression in several keys.

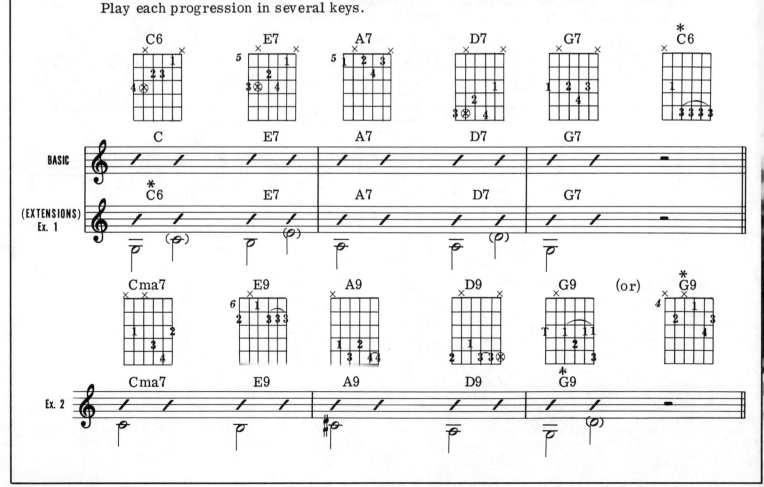

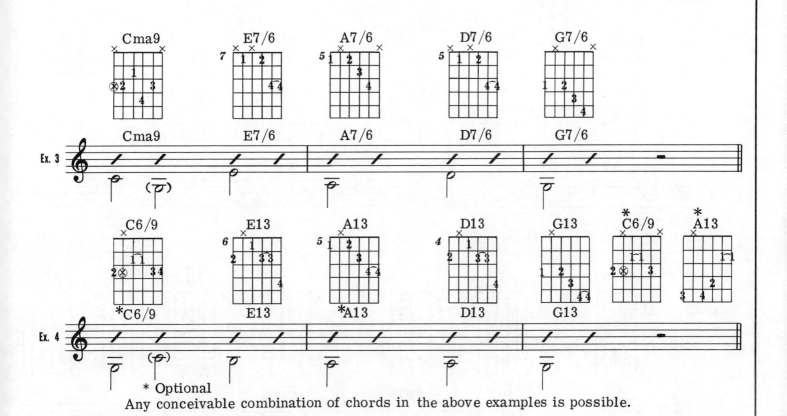

Ex. 3 — Cma9 | E7/6 | A7/6 | D7/6 | G7/6

Ex. 4 — *C6/9 | E13 | *A13 | D13 | G13

* Optional

Any conceivable combination of chords in the above examples is possible.

Chord Progression - G, B7, E7, A7, D7

Familiarize yourself thoroughly with all new chords in charts before attempting to play any of the examples in exercise below. Chords given are of the most popular ones.

Memorize and master thoroughly each chord progression example in the same procedure as before, moving up one fret chromatically each time applying same formation, etc. Play each progression in several keys.

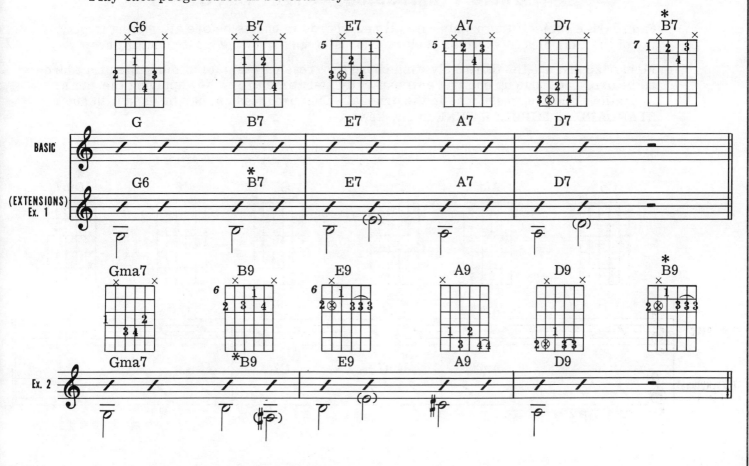

BASIC — G | B7 | E7 | A7 | D7

(EXTENSIONS) Ex. 1 — G6 | *B7 | E7 | A7 | D7

Ex. 2 — Gma7 | *B9 | E9 | A9 | D9

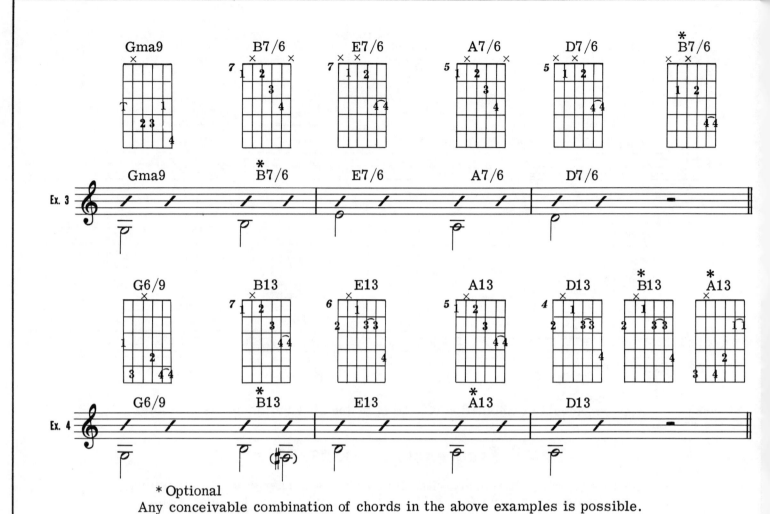

*Optional
Any conceivable combination of chords in the above examples is possible.

Chord Progression - C, Am, Dm, G7

Familiarize yourself thoroughly with all new chords in charts before attempting to play any of the examples in exercise below. Chords given are of the most popular ones.

Memorize and master thoroughly each chord progression example in the same procedure as before, and move up one fret chromatically each time to new key applying the same formations and progression as in the original. This progression may be used with any STANDARD or POPULAR TUNE in any key.

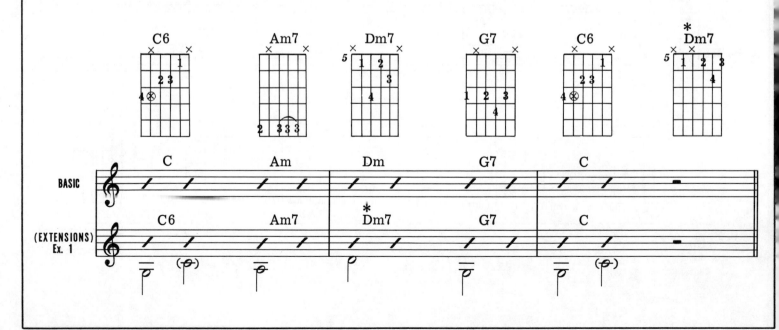

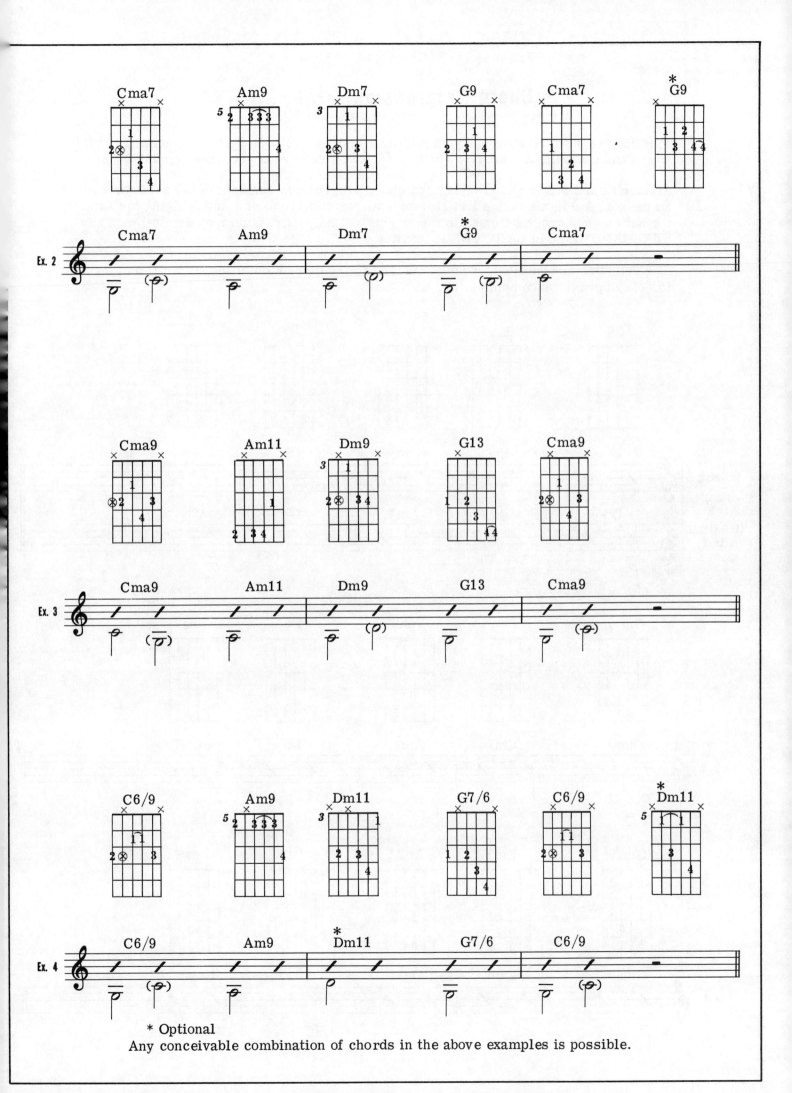

* Optional
Any conceivable combination of chords in the above examples is possible.

Chord Progression – G, Em, Am, D7

Familiarize yourself thoroughly with all new chords in charts before attempting to play any of the examples is exercise below. Chords given are of the most popular ones.

Memorize and master thoroughly each chord progression example in the same procedure as before, and move up one fret chromatically each time to new key applying the same formations and progression as in the original. This progression may be used with any STANDARD or POPULAR TUNE in any key.

The selection of tunes and/or songs is left to the discretion of the guitarist and teacher for chord progression application.

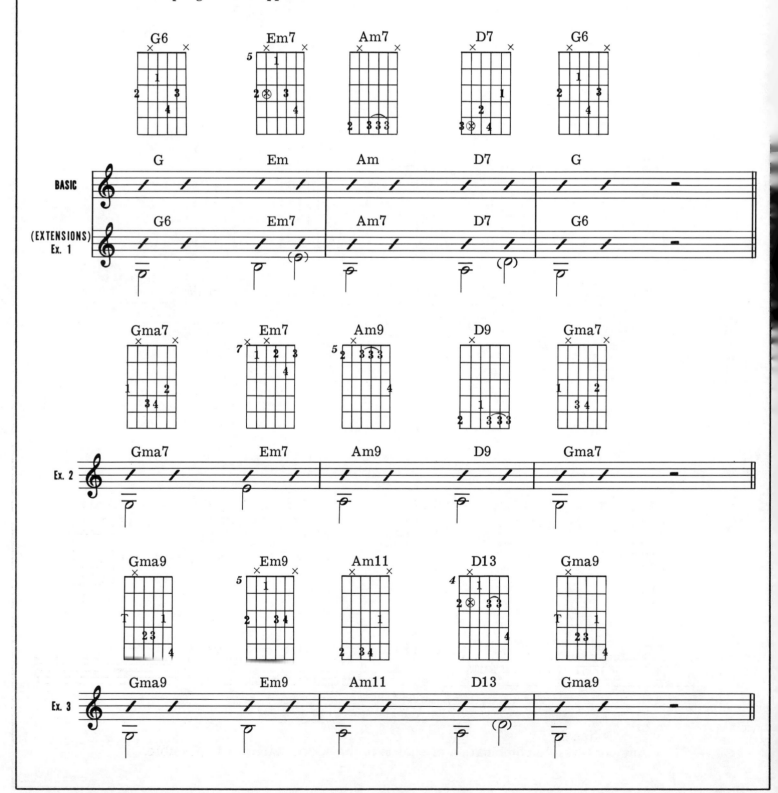

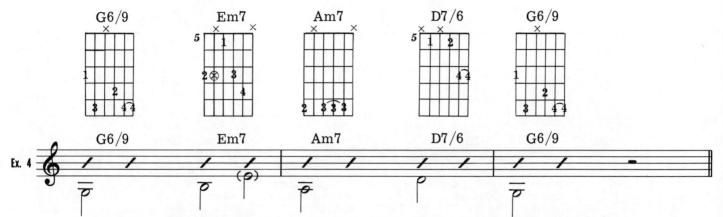

Any conceivable combination of chords in the above examples is possible.

Chord Progression - E♭, Cm, Fm, B♭7

Primarily, this study in chord progressions is based on two keys-namely C and G. However, a few chord progression exercises with examples in the key of E♭ are given to show what can be developed by using the movable formation system, i. e., move up one fret chromatically each time, applying the same formations and progression to the particular key desired. Ordinarily, the forms used here are the same as in the key of C, but to provide a better bass and treble line, we use forms other than in the original key. Proceed in the same manner as before, by playing the progression in several keys. This progression may be used with any standard or popular tune in any key.

Familiarize yourself thoroughly with all new chords in charts before attempting to play any of the examples in exercise below. Chords given are of the most popular ones.

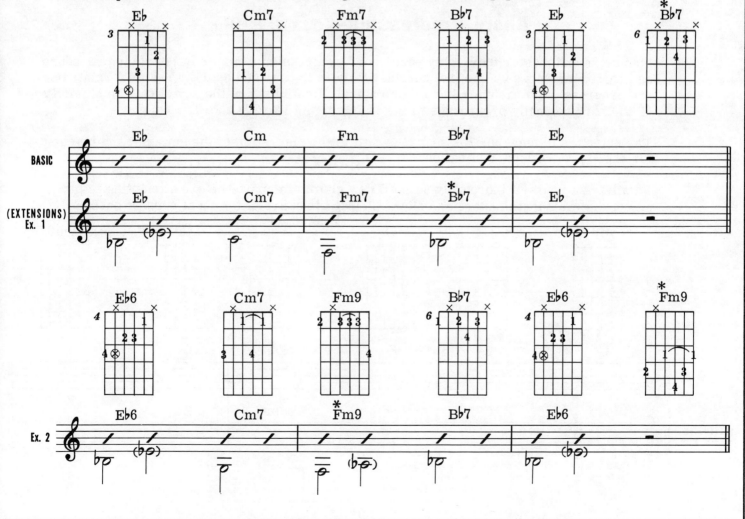

21

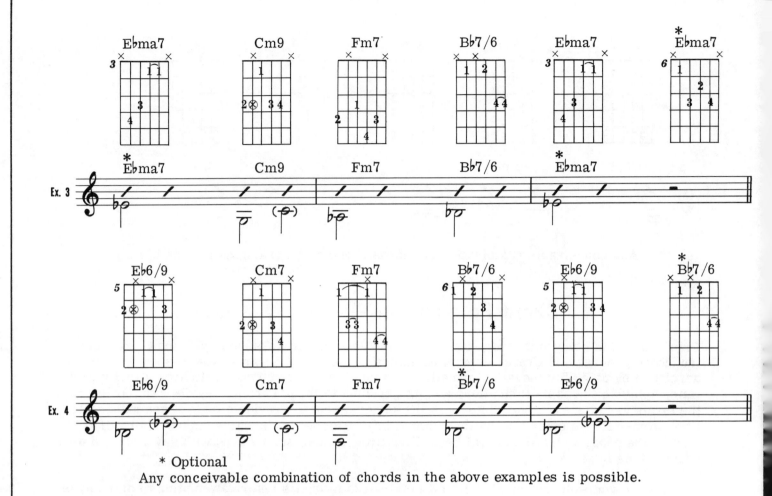

* Optional

Any conceivable combination of chords in the above examples is possible.

Chord Progression – C, C7, F, Fm

Memorize and master thoroughly each chord progression example in the same procedure as before, and move up one fret chromatically each time and apply the same formations and progression to each new key as in original. Continue thru the key of G. The Minor IV (Fm) chord normally progresses to the I, (C) or the V7 (G7) chord.

The selection of tunes and/or songs is left to the discretion of the guitarist and teacher for chord progression application.

Familiarize yourself thoroughly with all new chords in charts before attempting to play any of the examples in exercise below. Chords given are of the most popular ones.

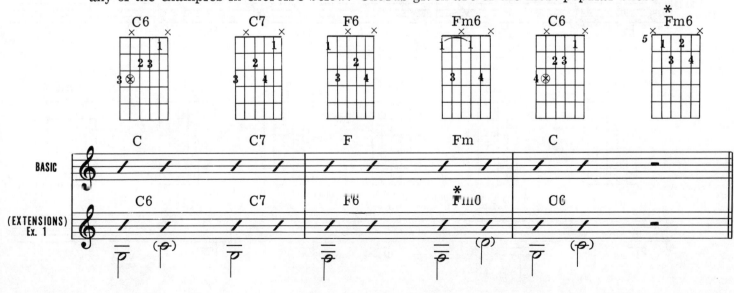

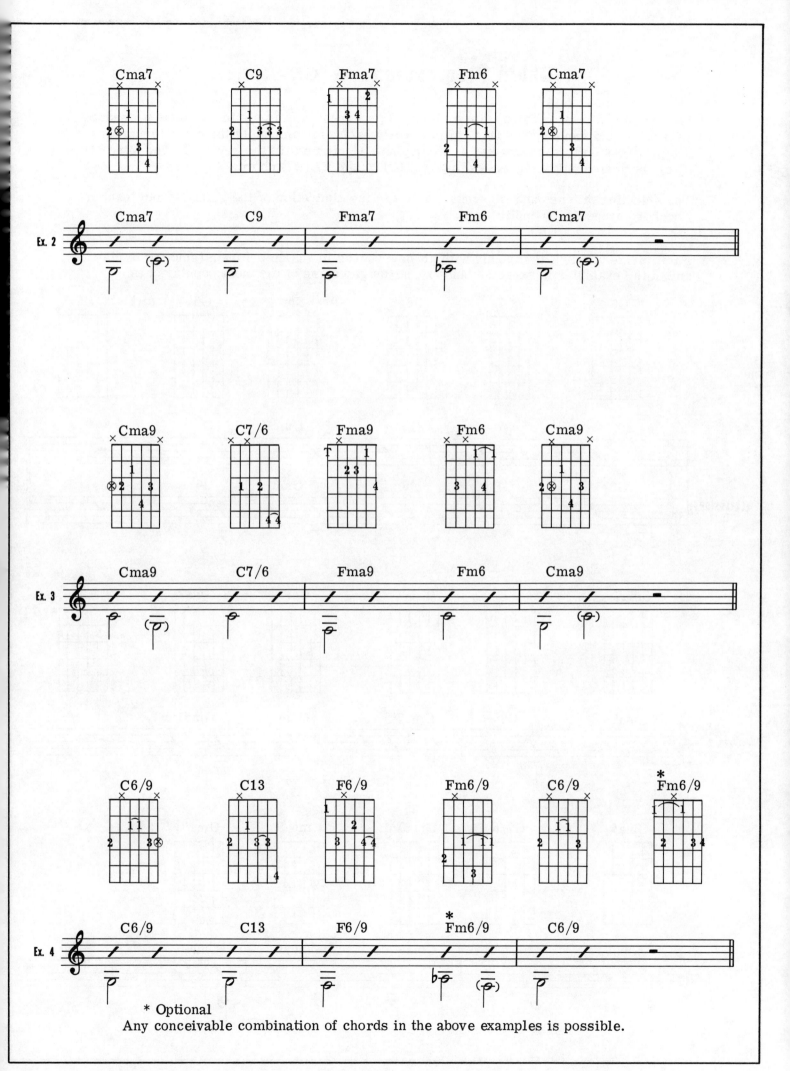

* Optional
Any conceivable combination of chords in the above examples is possible.

Chord Progression - G, G7, C, Cm

Memorize and master thoroughly each chord progression example in the same procedure as before, and move up one fret chromatically each time and apply the same formations and progression to each new key as in original. Continue thru the key of C. The Minor IV (Cm) chord normally progresses to the I, (C) or the V7 (D7) chord.

The selection of tunes and/or songs is left to the discretion of the guitarist and teacher for chord progression application.

Familiarize yourself thoroughly with all new chords in charts before attempting to play any of the examples in exercise below. Chords given are of the most popular ones.

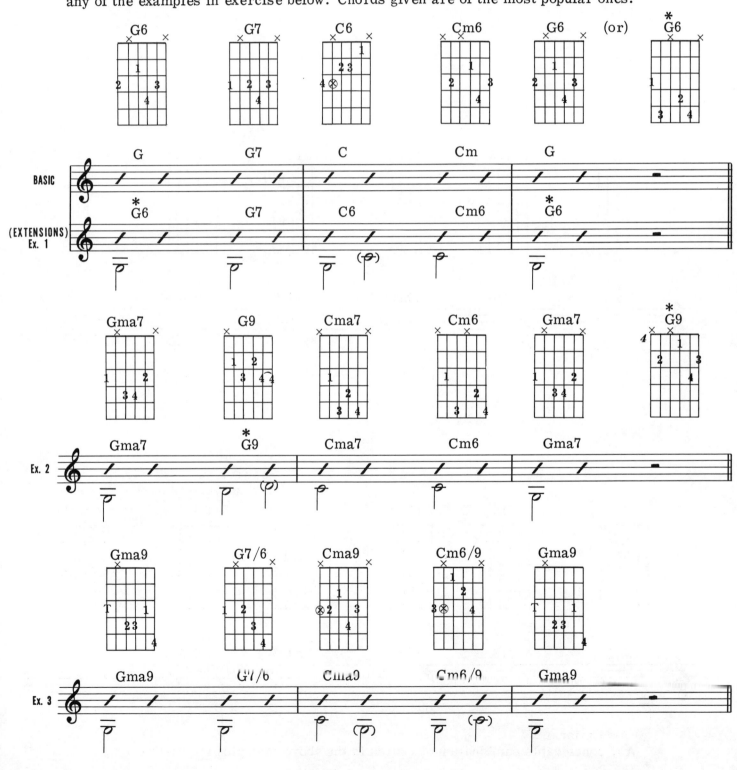

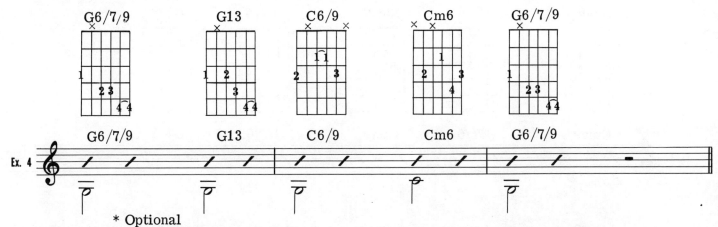

* Optional

Any conceivable combination of chords in the above examples is possible.

Chord Progression – C, C7, F, D7, G7

Memorize and master thoroughly each chord progression example in the same procedure as before, and move up one fret chromatically each time and apply the same formations and progression to new keys as in original. Play each progression in several keys.

The selection of tunes and/or songs is left to the discretion of the guitarist and teacher for chord progression application.

Familiarize yourself thoroughly with all new chords in charts before attempting to play any of the examples in exercise below. Chords given are of the most popular ones.

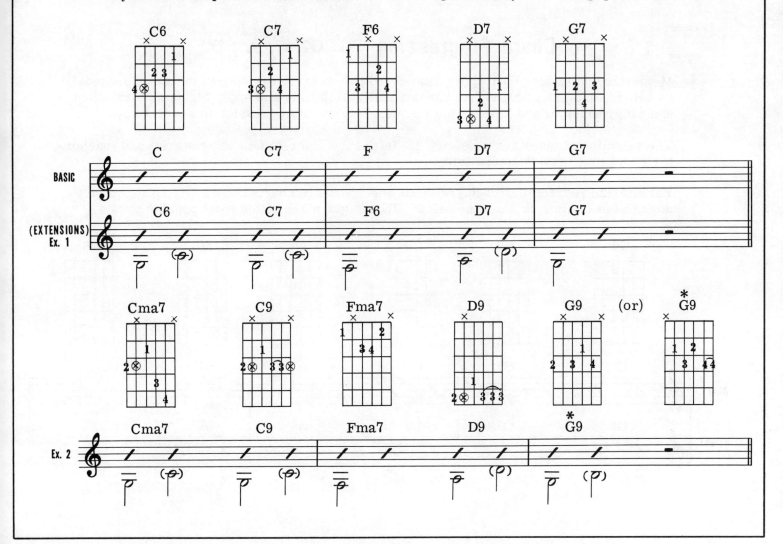

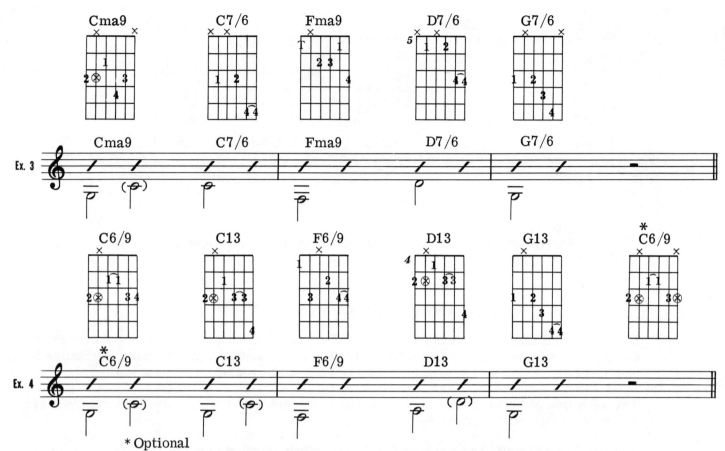

Ex. 3

Ex. 4

*Optional

Any conceivable combination of chords in the above examples is possible.

Chord Progression – G, G7, C, A7, D7

Memorize and master thoroughly each chord progression example in the same procedure as before, and move up one fret chromatically each time and apply the same formations and progression to new keys as in original. Play each progression in several keys.

The selection of tunes and/or songs is left to the discretion of the guitarist and teacher for chord progression application.

Familiarize yourself thoroughly with all new chords in charts before attempting to play any of the examples in exercise below. Chords given are of the most popular ones.

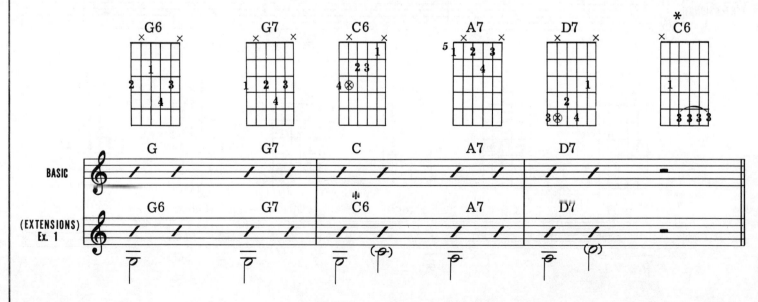

BASIC

(EXTENSIONS)
Ex. 1

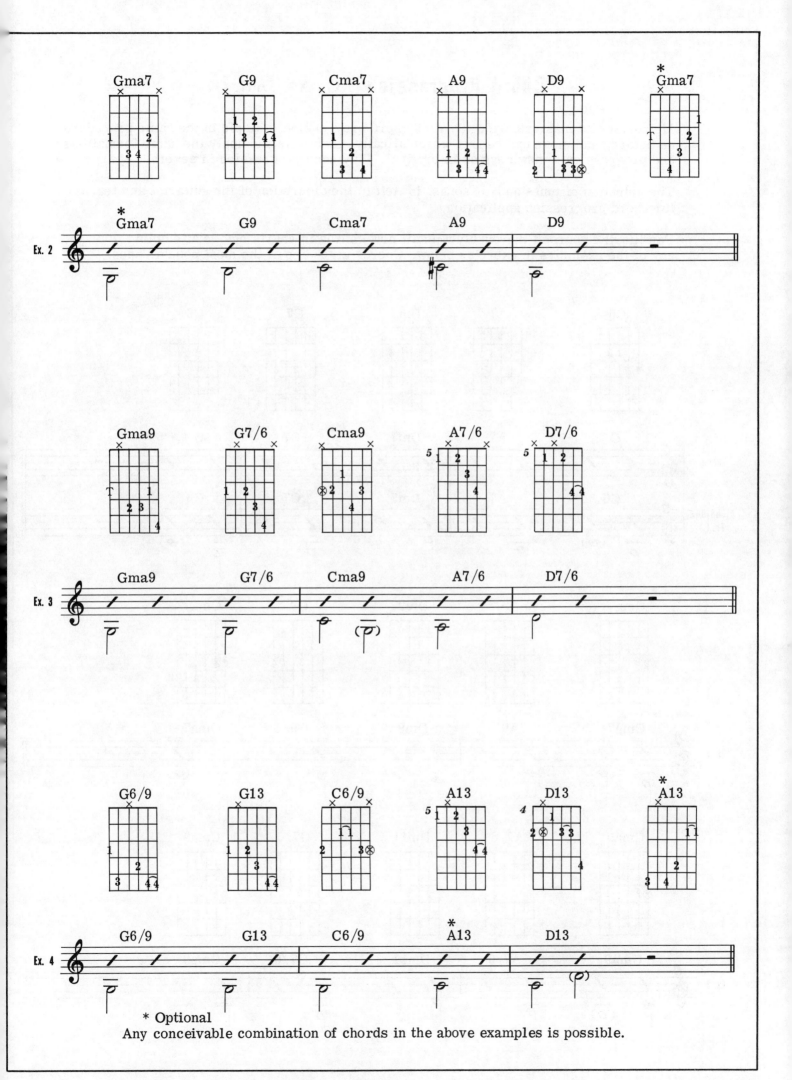

* Optional
Any conceivable combination of chords in the above examples is possible.

Chord Progression - C, A7, Dm7, G7

Memorize and master thoroughly each chord progression example in the same procedure as before, and move up one fret chromatically each time and apply the same formations and progression to new keys as in original. Play each progression in several keys.

The selection of tunes and/or songs is left to the discretion of the guitarist and teacher for chord progression application.

Familiarize yourself thoroughly with all new chords in charts before attempting to play any of the examples in exercise below. Chords given are of the most popular ones.

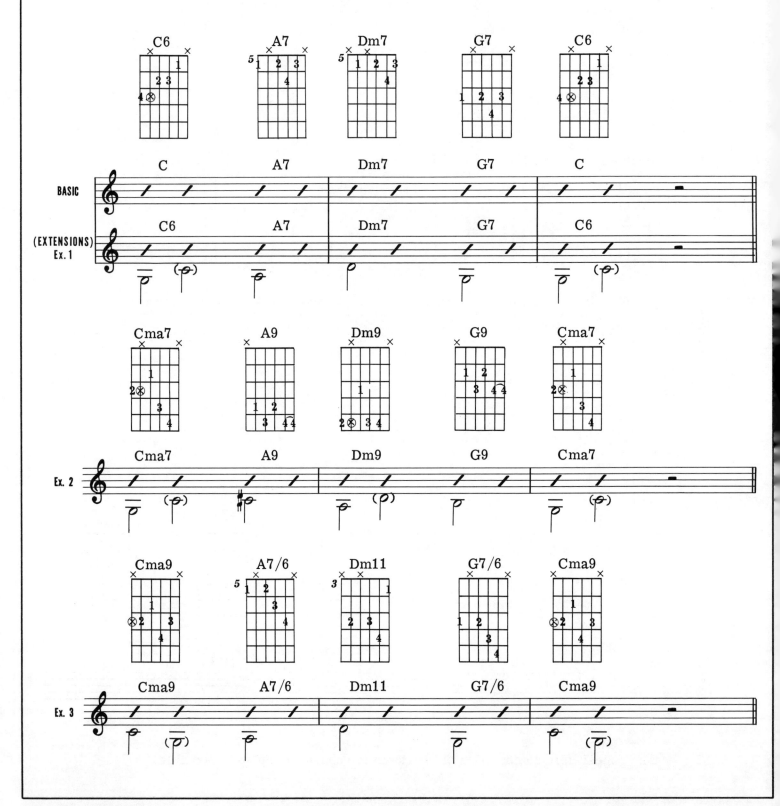

28

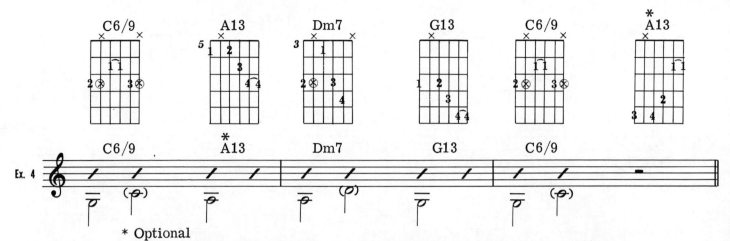

Any conceivable combination of chords in the above examples is possible.

Chord Progression – G, E7, Am7, D7

Memorize and master thoroughly each chord progression example in the same procedure as before, and move up one fret chromatically each time and apply the same formations and progression to new keys as in original. Play each progression in several keys.

The selection of tunes and/or songs is left to the discretion of the guitarist and teacher for chord progression application.

Familiarize yourself thoroughly with all new chords in charts before attempting to play any of the examples in exercise below. Chords given are of the most popular ones.

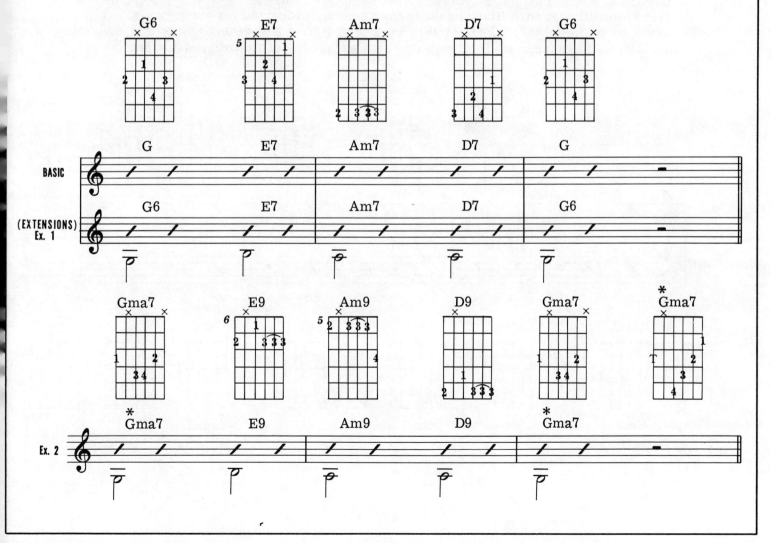

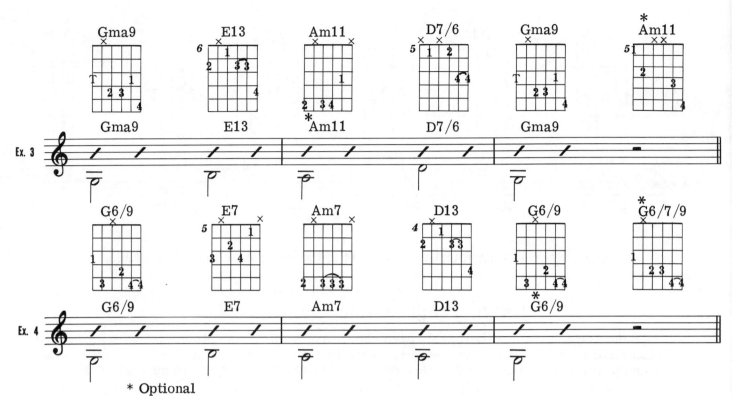

Ex. 3

Ex. 4

* Optional

Any conceivable combination of chords in the above examples is possible.

Chord Progression – C, C♯dim.7, Dm7, G7

In this standard progression, the chromatic diminished 7th chord progresses 1/2 step upward to a minor 7th chord. Continue the same procedure as before by moving up one fret chromatically each time and apply the same chord formations and progression to new keys as in original. Continue thru the key of G. The selection of tunes and/or songs is left to the discretion of the guitarist and teacher for chord progression application.

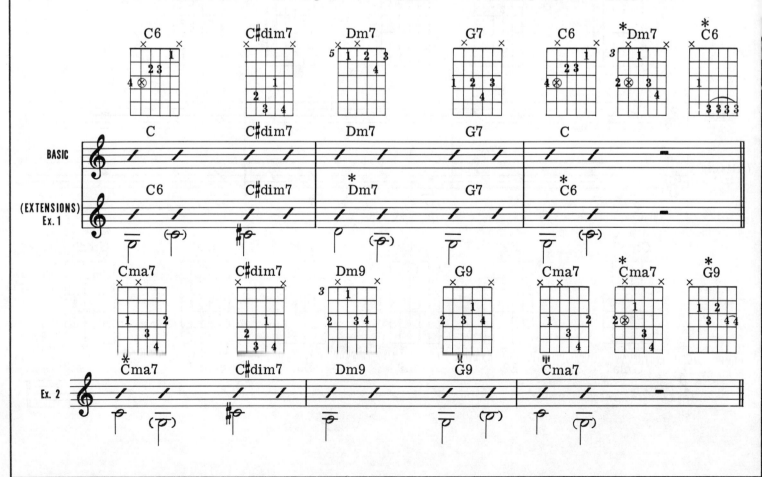

BASIC

(EXTENSIONS)
Ex. 1

Ex. 2

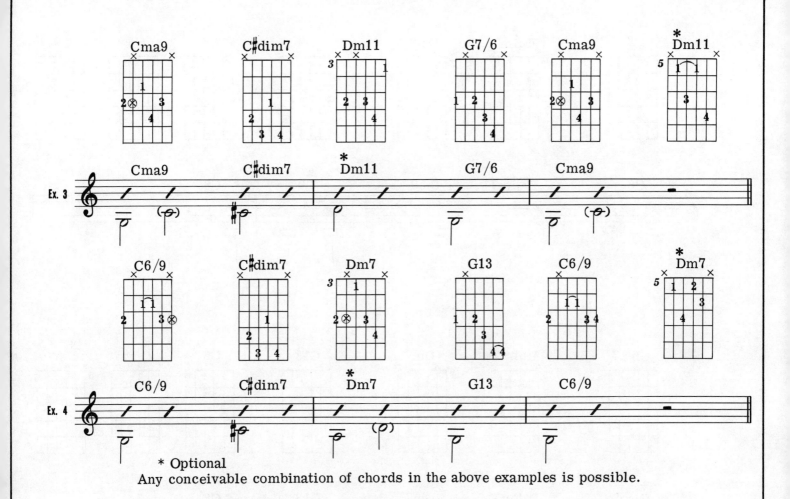

Ex. 3

Ex. 4

* Optional

Any conceivable combination of chords in the above examples is possible.

Chord Progression – C, E♭dim.7, Dm7, G7

In this standard progression, the chromatic diminished 7th chord progresses downward 1/2 step to a minor 7th chord. Continue the same procedure as before, by moving up one fret chromatically each time, and apply the same formations and progression to new keys as in original. Continue thru the key of G.

Familiarize yourself thoroughly with all new chords in charts before attempting to play any of the examples in exercise below. Chords given are of the most popular ones.

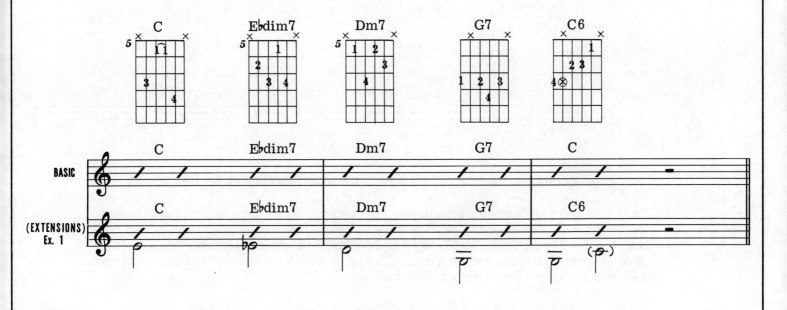

BASIC

(EXTENSIONS)
Ex. 1

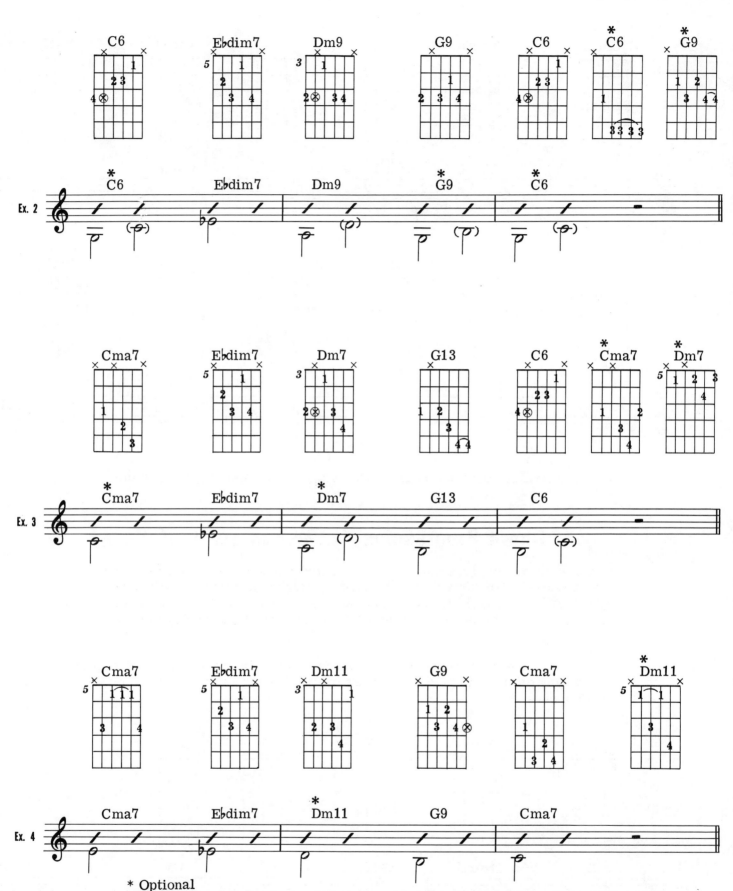

* Optional

Any conceivable combination of chords in the above examples is possible.

Now that you are familiar with the two preceding chromatic diminished 7th chord progressions, combine the two together and note how you achieve a pleasant bass and treble-line pattern. Examples can be played in any conceivable combination. The selection of tunes and/or songs is left to the discretion of the guitarist and teacher for chord progression application.

Chord Progression – G, G#dim.7, Am7, D7

In this standard progression, the chromatic diminished 7th chord progresses 1/2 step upward to a minor 7th chord. Continue the same procedure as before by moving up one fret chromatically each time, and apply the same chord formations and progression to new keys as in original. Continue thru the key of C.

Familiarize yourself thoroughly with all new chords in charts before attempting to play any of the examples in exercise below. Chords given are of the most popular ones.

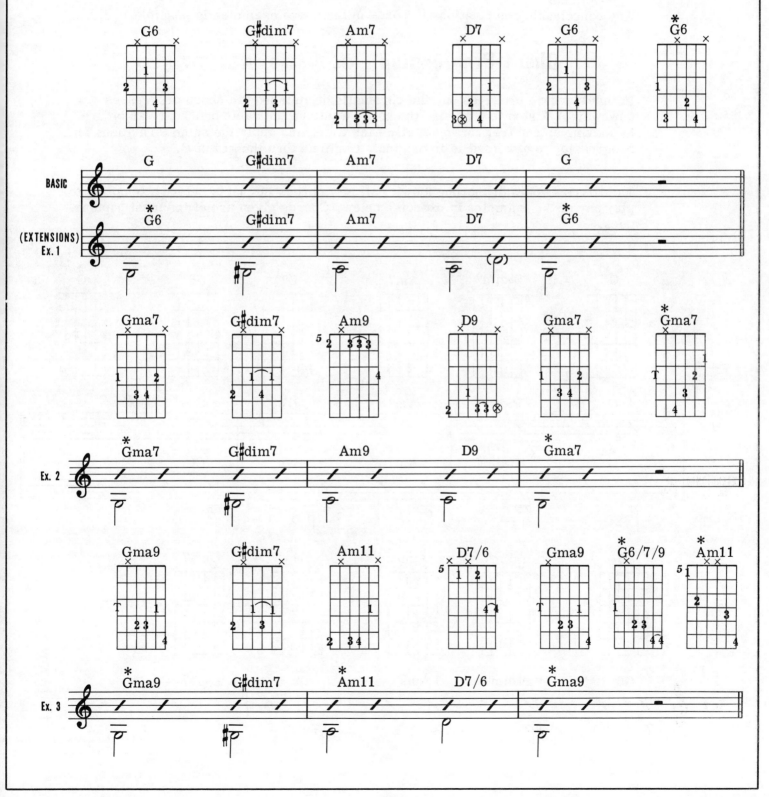

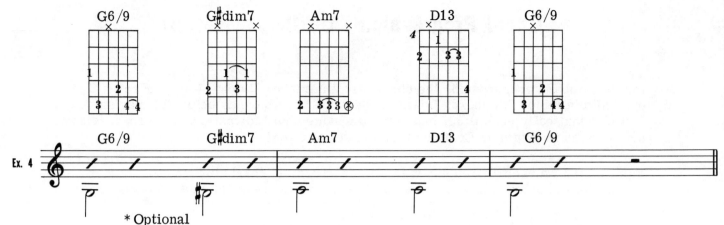

*Optional

Any conceivable combination of chords in the above examples is possible.

Chord Progression – G, B♭dim.7, Am7, D7

In this standard progression, the chromatic diminished 7th chord progresses downward 1/2 step to a minor 7th chord. Continue the same procedure as before, by moving up one fret chromatically each time, and apply the same formations and progression to new keys as in original. Continue thru the key of C.

Familiarize yourself thoroughly with all new chrods in charts before attempting to play any of the examples in exercise below. Chords given are of the most popular ones.

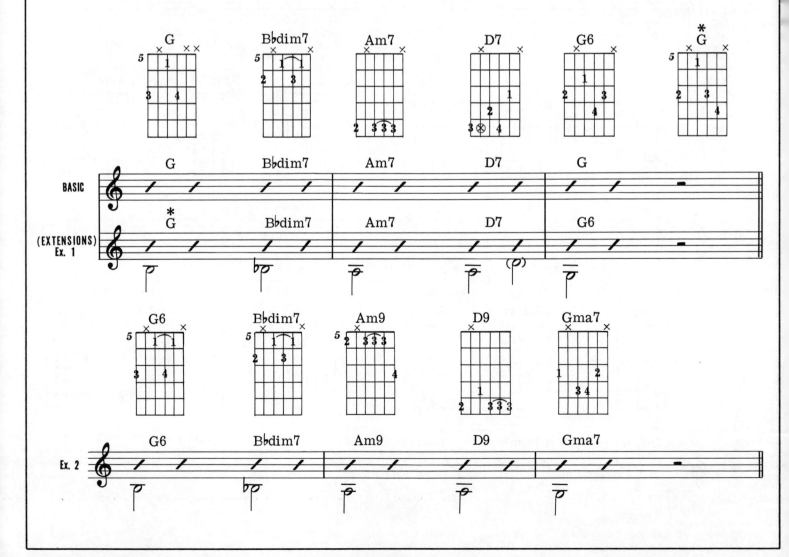

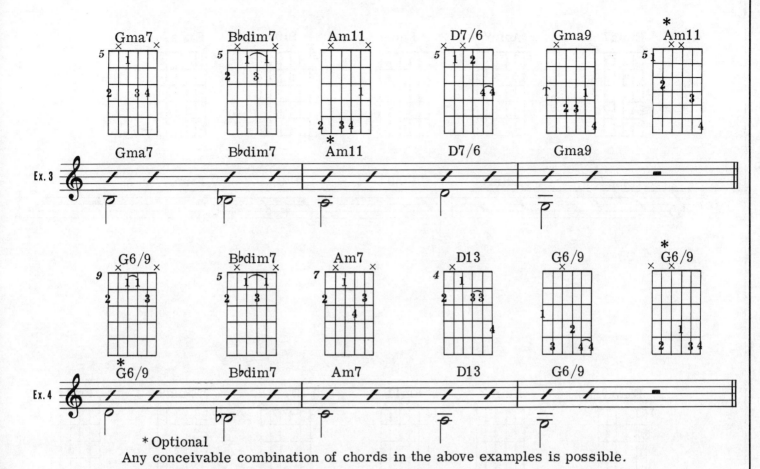

*Optional

Any conceivable combination of chords in the above examples is possible.

Combine the two chromatic diminished 7th chord progressions as before. Any conceivable combination of chords in the combined examples is possible.

Chord Progression - E♭, Adim.7, Fm7, B♭7

Again we use the key of E♭. Let's see what can be developed with the chromatic diminished 7th chord, using the principle of moving up one fret chromatically each time to the particular key desired, applying the same formations and progression as in the original key. To provide a better bass line, we use forms other than the originals. Listen to the chords and progressions to establish the different chordal tonalities thoroughly in your ear. The selection of tunes and/or songs is left to the discretion of the guitarist and teacher for chord progression application.

Familiarize yourself thoroughly with all new chords in charts before attempting to play any of the examples in exercise below. Chords given are of the most popular ones.

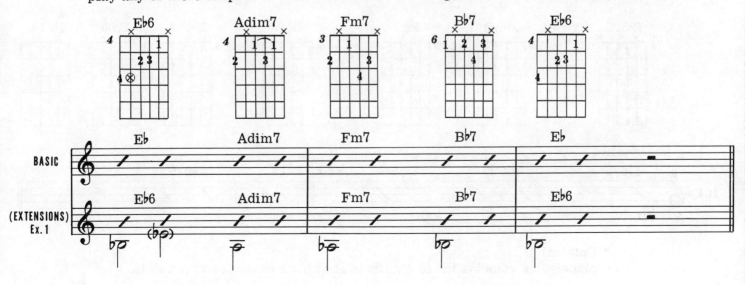

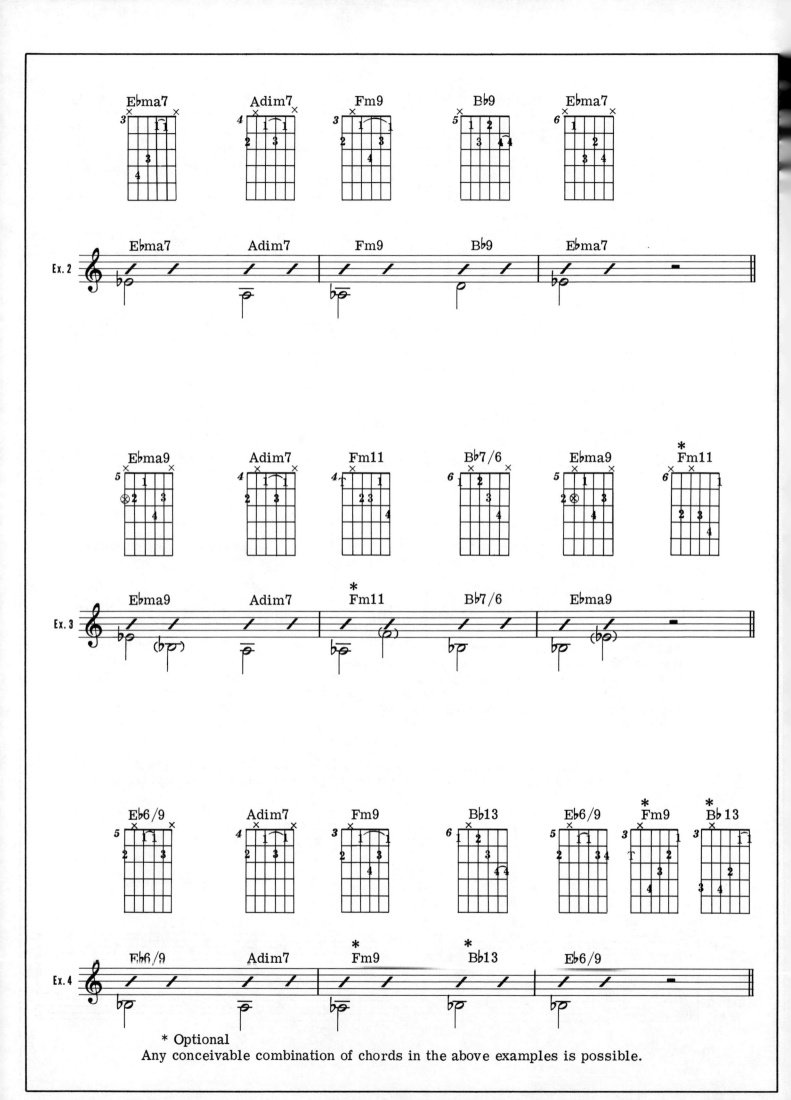

* Optional
Any conceivable combination of chords in the above examples is possible.

Review

COMBINED COMBINATIONS

C, C#dim.7, Dm7, G7
C, Ebdim.7, Dm7, G7
C, C7, F, Fm

Here we have three previous chord progressions combined in a review to show how a combination of progressions form a typical popular progression found in many tunes and/or songs utilizing several combinations.

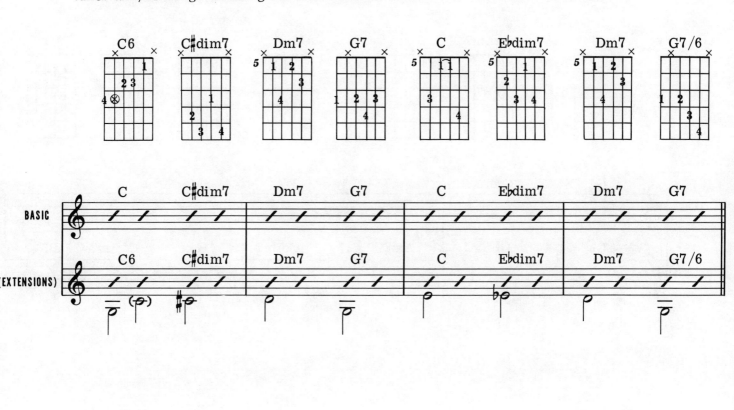

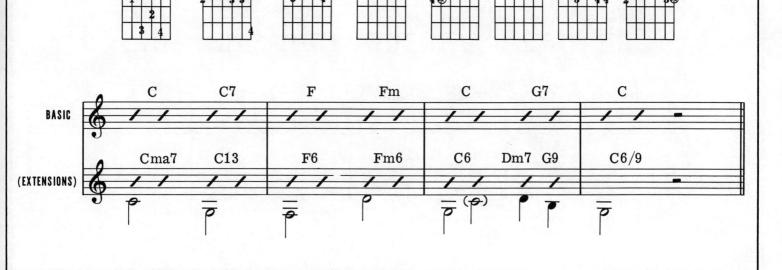

37

Review

COMBINED COMBINATIONS

G, G#dim. 7, Am7, D7
G, G7,   C, Cm
G, Bdim. 7, Am7, D7

Here we have three chord progressions combined with some variations. Note the basic given and see how a combination provides a typical sequence found in many popular tunes when properly utilized with extensions.

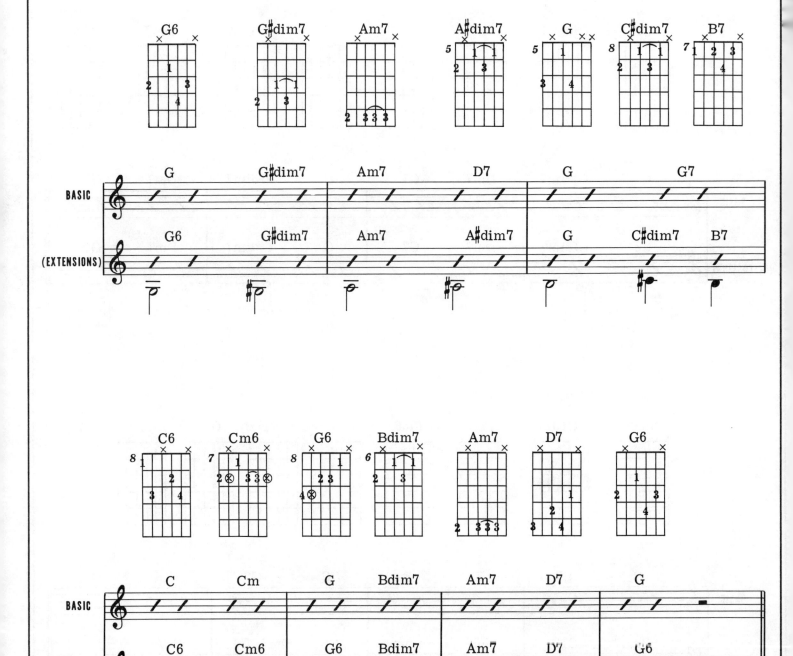

Chord Progression - C, Gm6, A7, Dm7, G7

Memorize and master thoroughly each chord progression example in the same procedure as before, and move up one fret chromatically each time and apply the same formations and progression to each new key as in original. Continue thru the key of G.

Familiarize yourself thoroughly with all new chords in charts before attempting to play any of the examples in exercise below. Chords given are of the most popular ones.

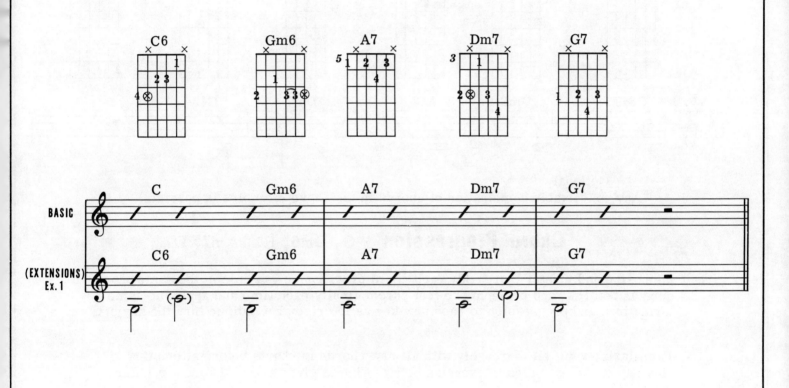

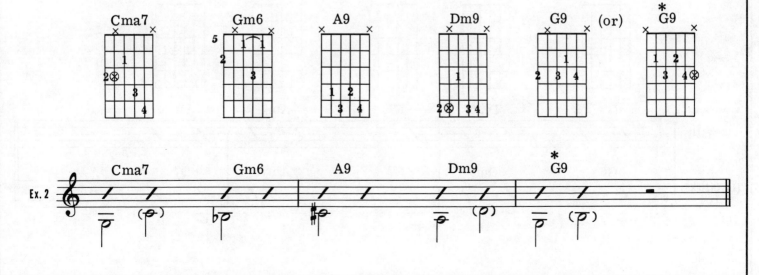

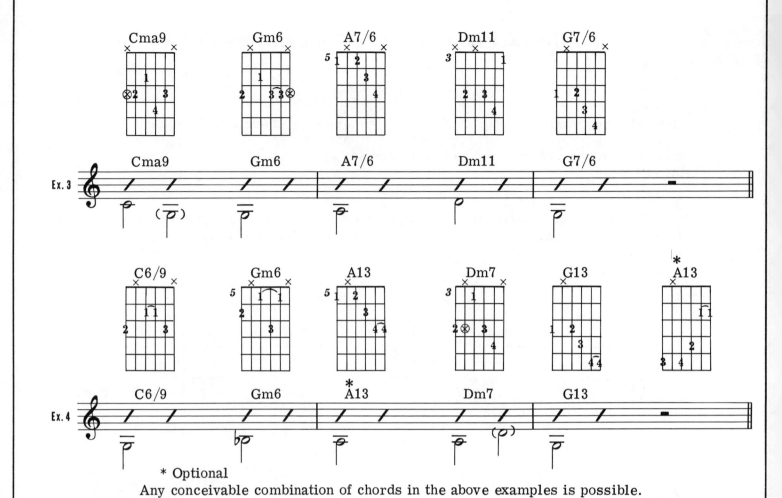

* Optional

Any conceivable combination of chords in the above examples is possible.

Chord Progression - G, Dm6, E7, Am7, D7

Memorize and master thoroughly each chord progression example in the same procedure as before, and move up one fret chromatically each time and apply the same formations and progression to each new key as in original. Continue thru the key of C.

Familiarize yourself thoroughly with all new chords in charts before attempting to play any of the examples in exercise below. Chords given are of the most popular ones.

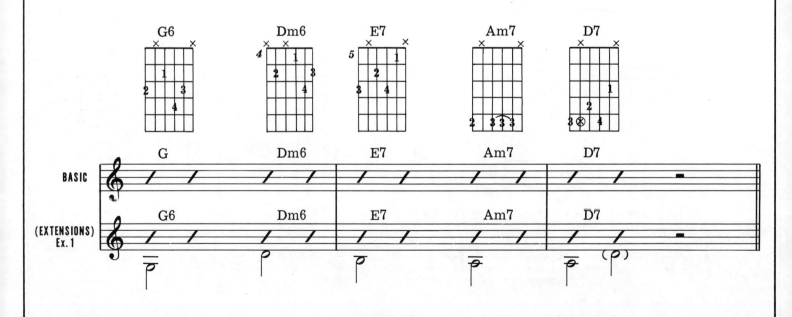

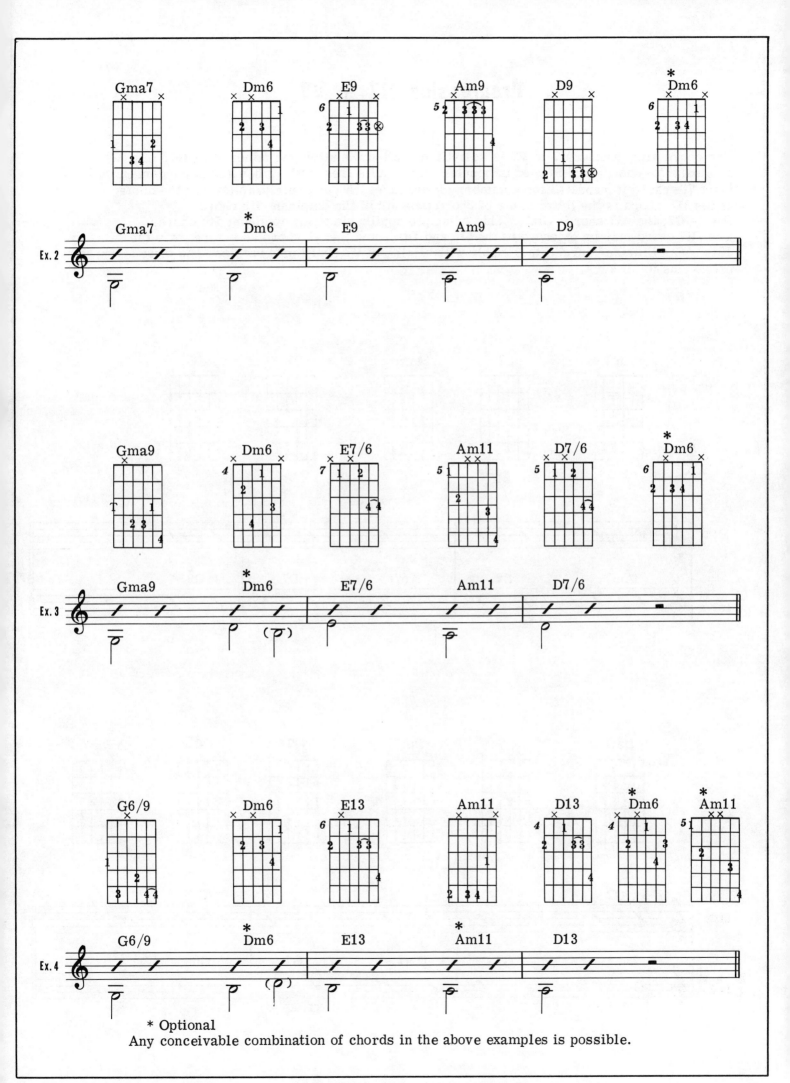

* Optional
Any conceivable combination of chords in the above examples is possible.

Progression II7 to V7

The chord progression II7 to V7 is sometimes called the alternate minor 7th chord of a dominant 7th chord, and is used in popular music quite frequently when the same dominant 7th chord is repeated for a number of measures. A good rule to follow for the name of the II7 chord is the letter name of chord tone 5th of the dominant 7th chord. (Ex. - C7; the II7 chord, Gm7). This principle applicable to all dominant 7th chords. The II7 chord may be extended to the 9th and 11th, and the V7 chord as before; thru the 13th. Familiarize yourself thoroughly with all II7 to V7 chord progressions and their extensions in all keys.

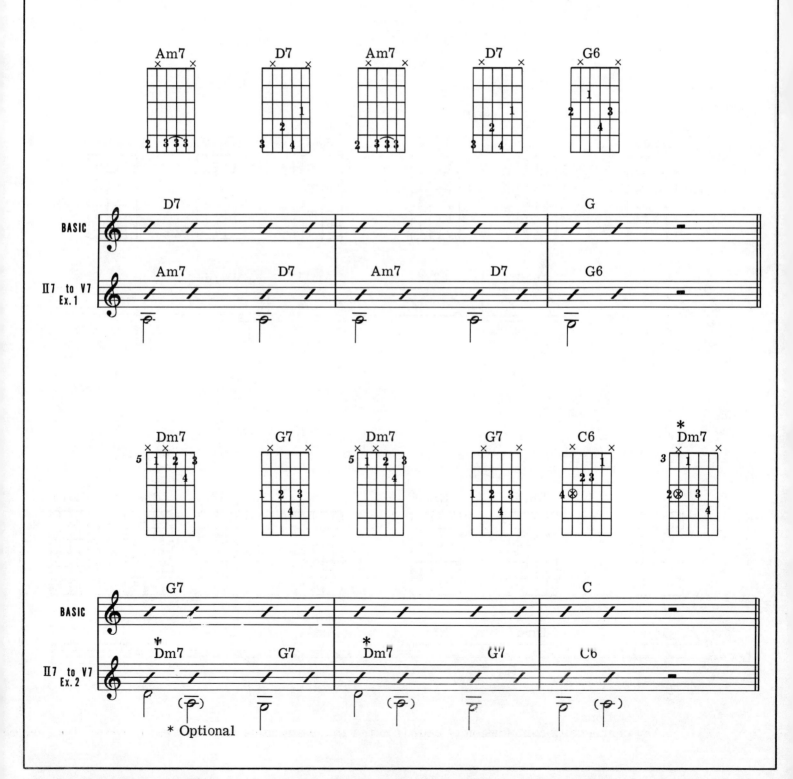

* Optional

The III Chord

The III chord of a key is frequently used in modern progressions, and is generally used as a passing-chord or substitute-chord when the I chord is repeated for a number of measures. A useful progression is the sequence of diatonic chords progressing from the I chord of a key up to the III chord, and back to the I chord. Note the movement of the bass-line. When the III chord is used in a scalewise progression. it's better not to extend it beyond the minor 7th.

Chord Progression – C, Dm, Em, Dm

Memorize and master thoroughly each chord progression example in the same procedure as before, and move up one fret chromatically each time to new key applying the same formations and progression as in original. Continue thru the key of G.

Familiarize yourself thoroughly with all new chords in charts before attempting to play any of the examples in exercise below. Chords given are of the most popular ones.

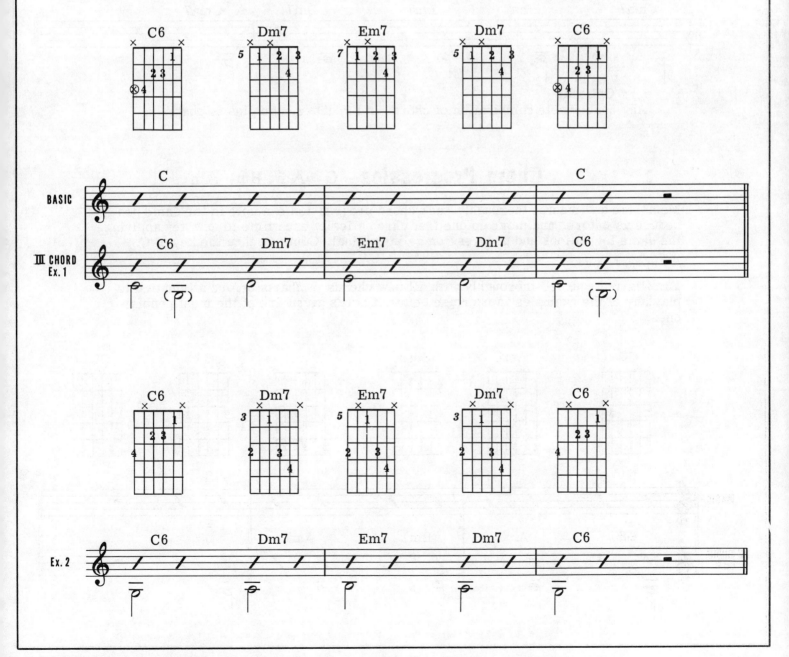

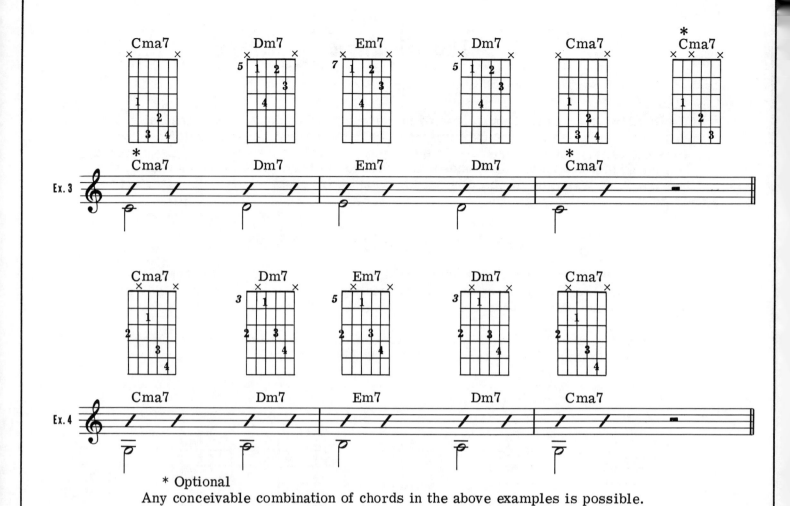

* Optional

Any conceivable combination of chords in the above examples is possible.

Chord Progression - G, Am, Bm, Am

Memorize and master thoroughly each chord progression example in the same procedure as before, and move up one fret chromatically each time to new key applying the same formations and progression as in original. Continue thru the key of C.

Familiarize yourself thoroughly with all new chords in charts before attempting to play any of the examples in exercise below. Chords given are of the most popular ones.

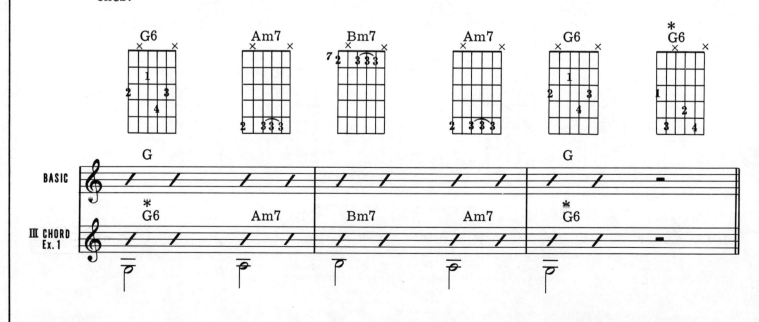

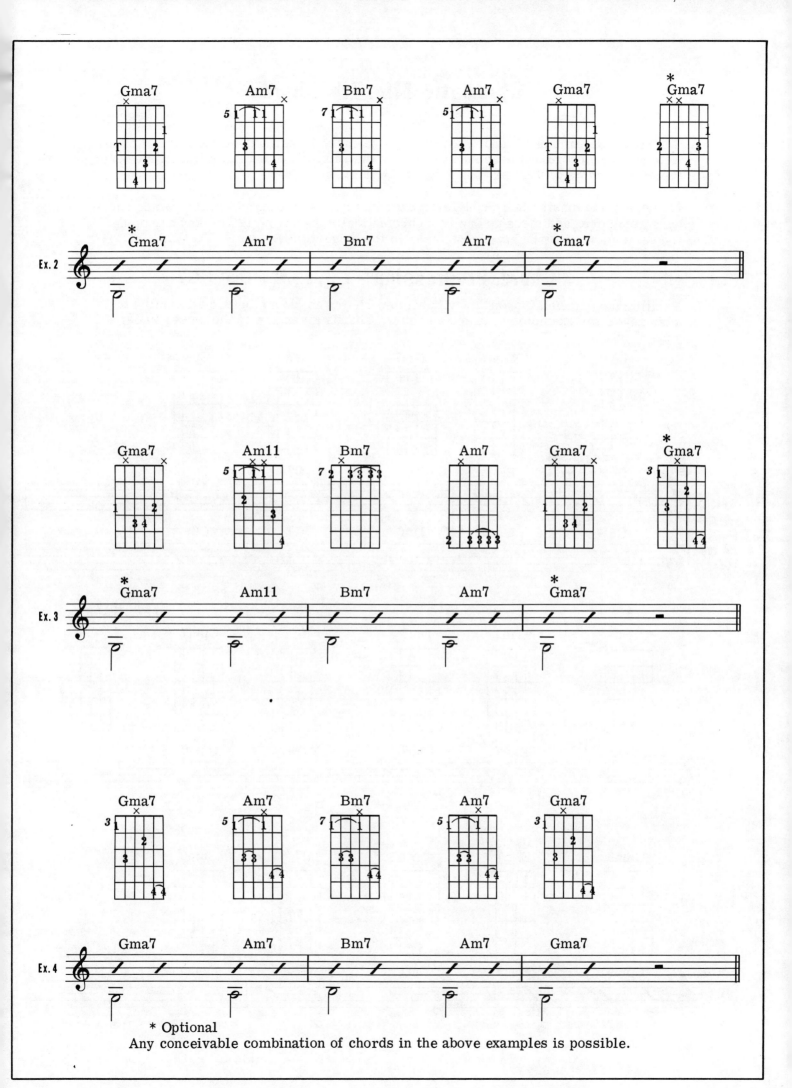

* Optional
Any conceivable combination of chords in the above examples is possible.

Chromatic Min. 7th Chords

The chromatic minor 7th chord normally progresses 1/2 step downward to a II chord. Note how this chord has been substituted for the Dim. 7th chord in the basic. However, the basic may be preferred; this is up to the individual.

Memorize and master thoroughly each chord progression example in the same procedure as before, and move up one fret chromatically each time to new key and apply the same formations and progression as in the original key.

Chord Progression - C6, E♭m7, Dm7, G7

Familiarize yourself thoroughly with all new chords in charts before attempting to play any of the examples in exercise below. Chords given are of the most popular ones.

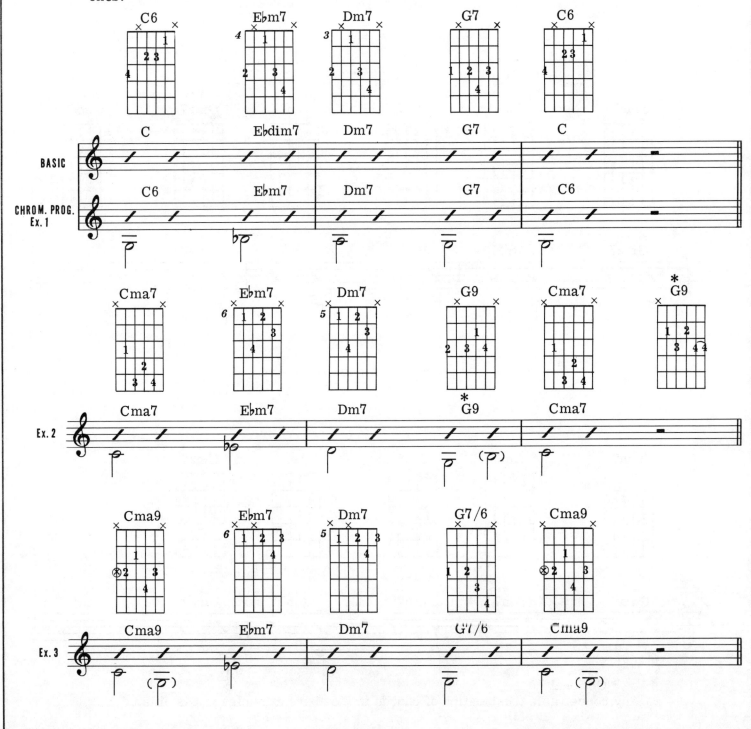

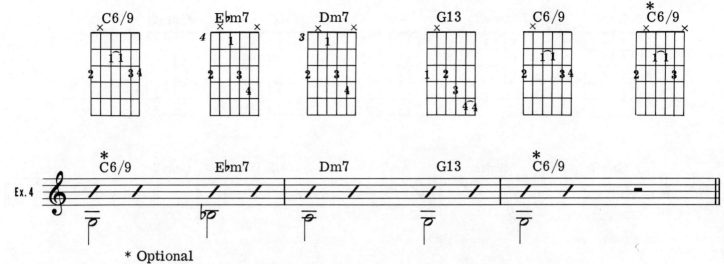

* Optional

Any conceivable combination of chords in the above examples is possible.

Chord Progression - G6, B♭m7, Am7, D7

Familiarize yourself thoroughly with all new chords in charts before attempting to play any of the examples in exercise below. Chords given are of the most popular ones.

Memorize and master thoroughly each chord progression example in the same procedure as before, and move up one fret chromatically each time to new key and apply the same formations and progression as in the original key.

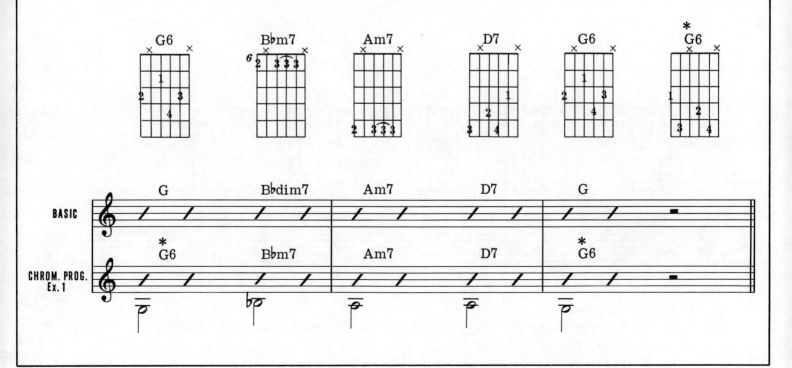

47

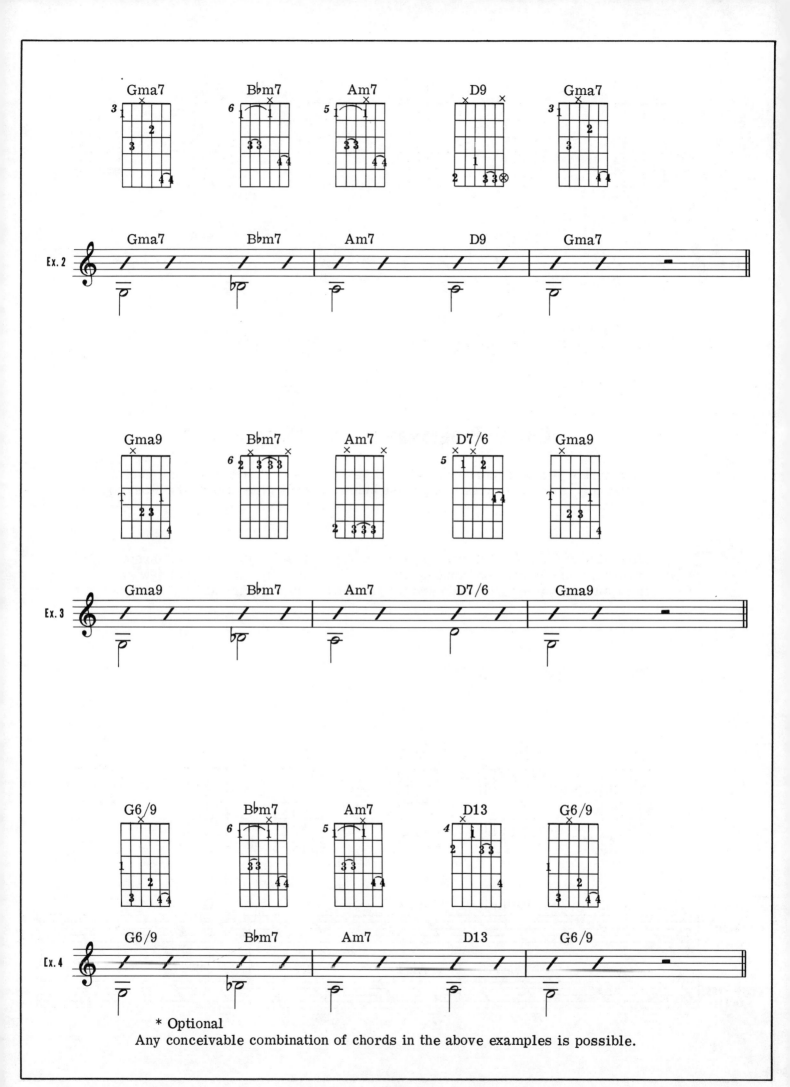

* Optional
Any conceivable combination of chords in the above examples is possible.

48

Chord Progression – C6, Dm7, Em7, E♭m7, Dm7, G7

Familiarize yourself thoroughly with all new chords in charts before attempting to play any of the examples in exercise below. Chords given are of the most popular ones.

Memorize and master thoroughly each chord progression example in the same procedure as before, moving up one fret chromatically each time applying same formation, etc. Play each progression in several keys.

This progression may be used with any STANDARD or POPULAR TUNE in any key.

Only two (2) examples are given in the chord progression exercise below, but continue with other extensions of each type chord except the III chord as in previous examples.

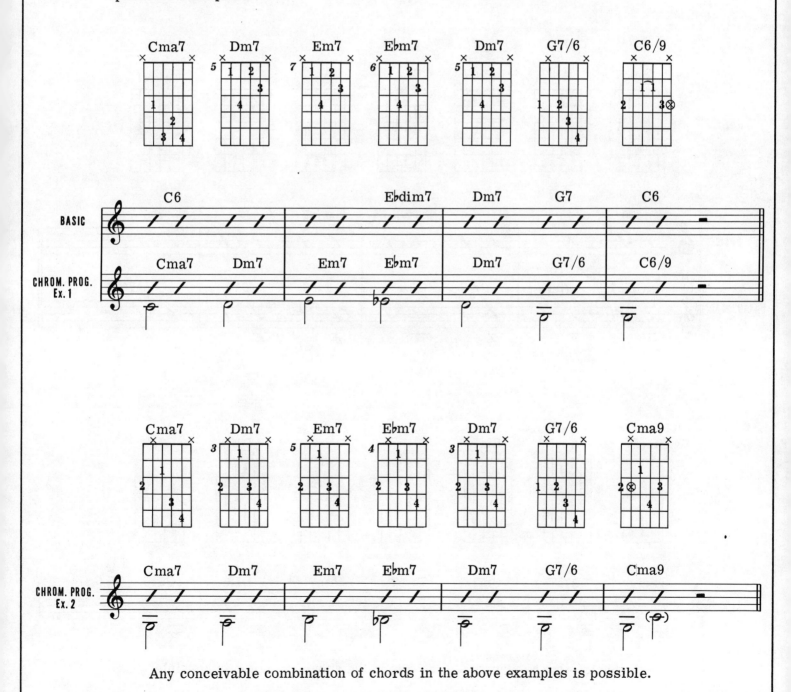

Any conceivable combination of chords in the above examples is possible.

Chord Progression - G6, Am7, Bm7, Bbm7, Am7, D7

Familiarize yourself thoroughly with all new chords in charts before attempting to play any of the examples in exercise below. Chords given are of the most popular ones. Only two (2) examples are given in the chord progression exercise below, but continue with other extensions of each type chord except the III chord as in previous examples. This progression may be used with any STANDARD or POPULAR TUNE in any key.

Memorize and master thoroughly each chord progression example in the same procedure as before, moving up one fret chromatically each time applying same formations, etc. Play each progression in several keys.

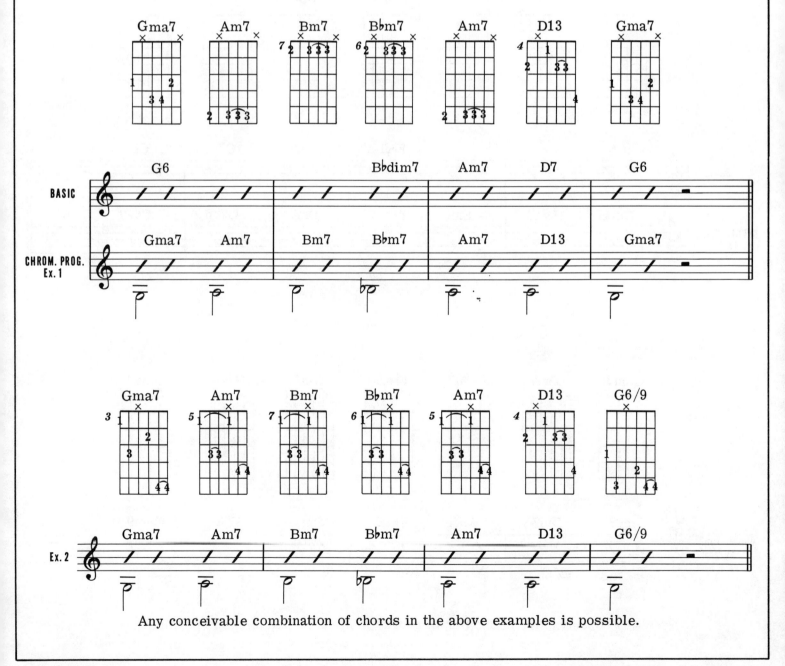

Any conceivable combination of chords in the above examples is possible.

Review—Blues Progression

In this review, based on the familiar Blues Progression, the II7 chord, the III7 chord and the chromatic minor 7th chord is illustrated. Note the difference in chords actually played from the ones given in the basic chord progression. This type of blues progression applies to any key.

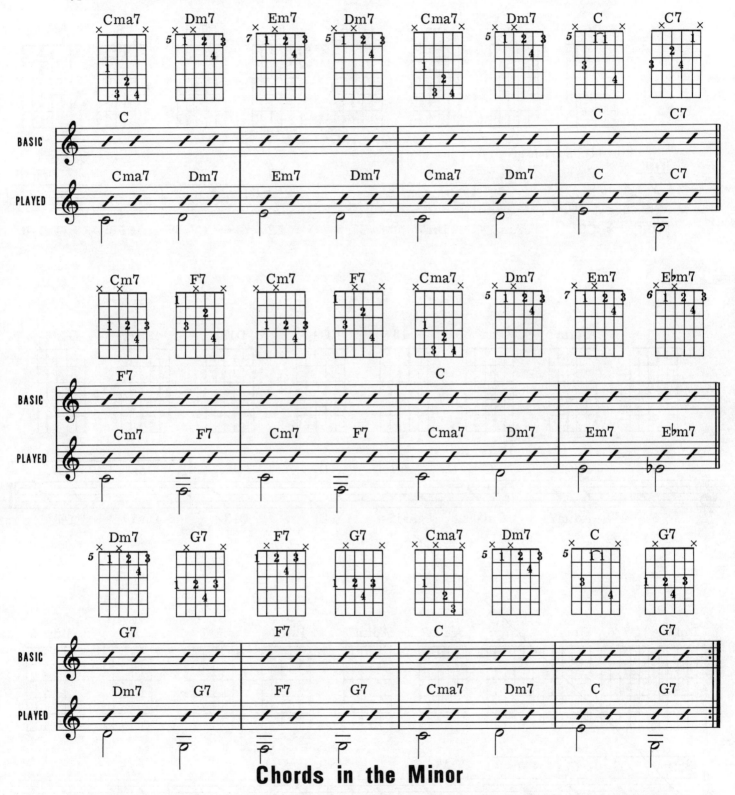

Chords in the Minor

The most important chords in a minor key are the I, IV, and V7 chords. For example: In the key of C minor Cm (I), Fm (IV), G7 (V7). The normal progression of these chords in the minor are the same as they are in major keys. For fullness, the chord tone 6th may be added to the I and IV chords of a key, and for the V7 chord, it may be extended thru the 13th as previously for dominant type chords.

Modern Chord Progression

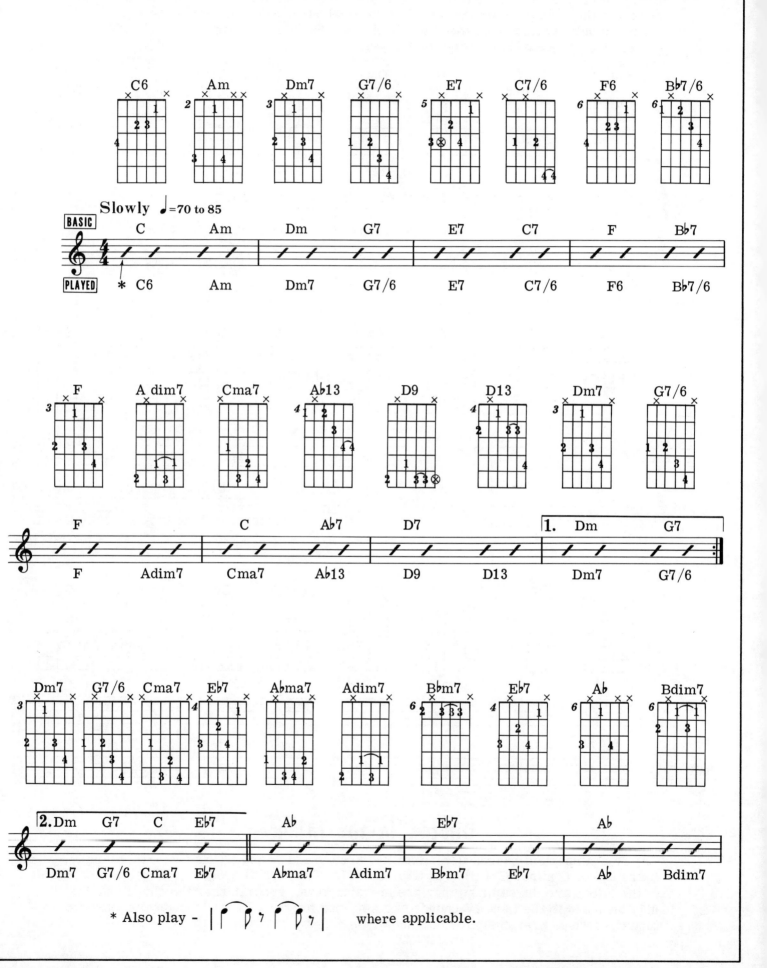

* Also play — where applicable.

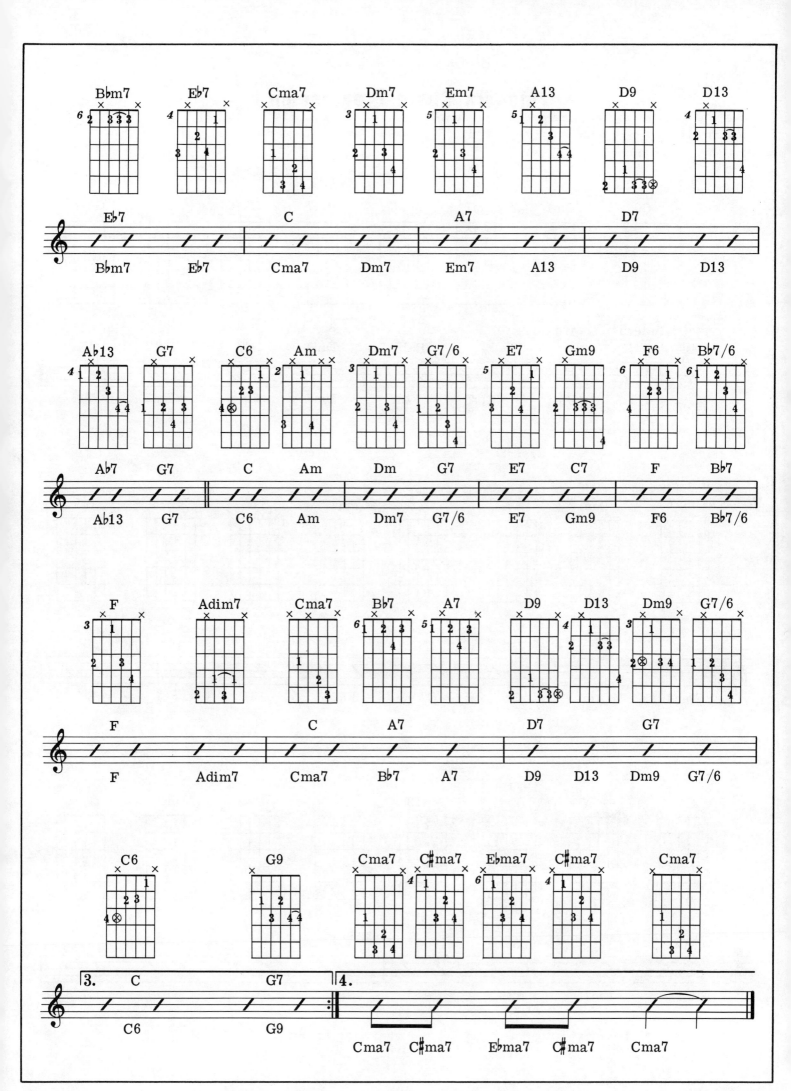

Modern Chord Progression

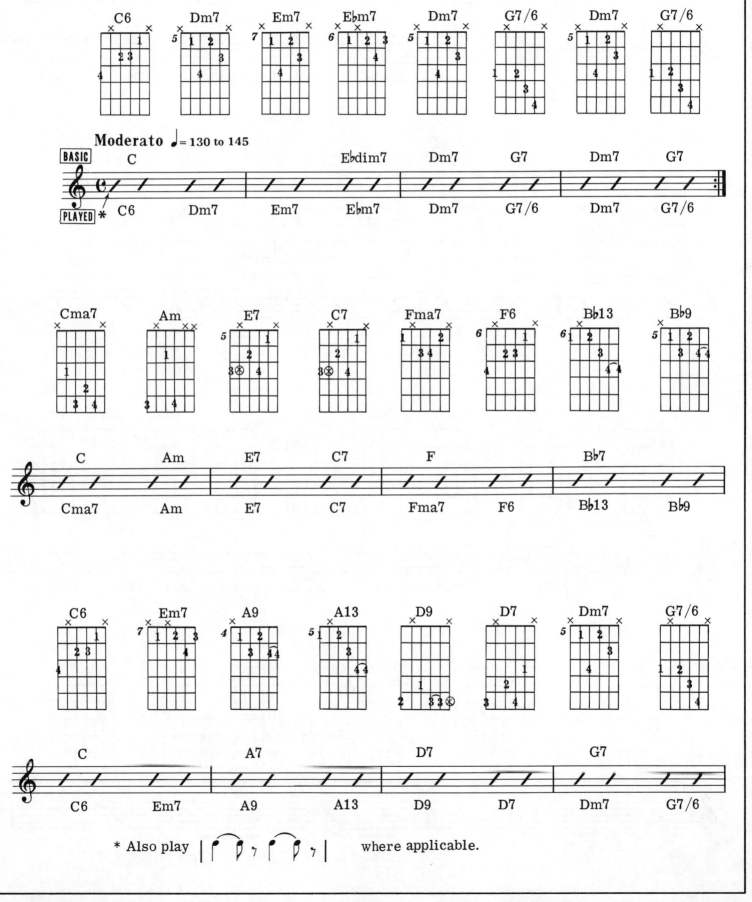

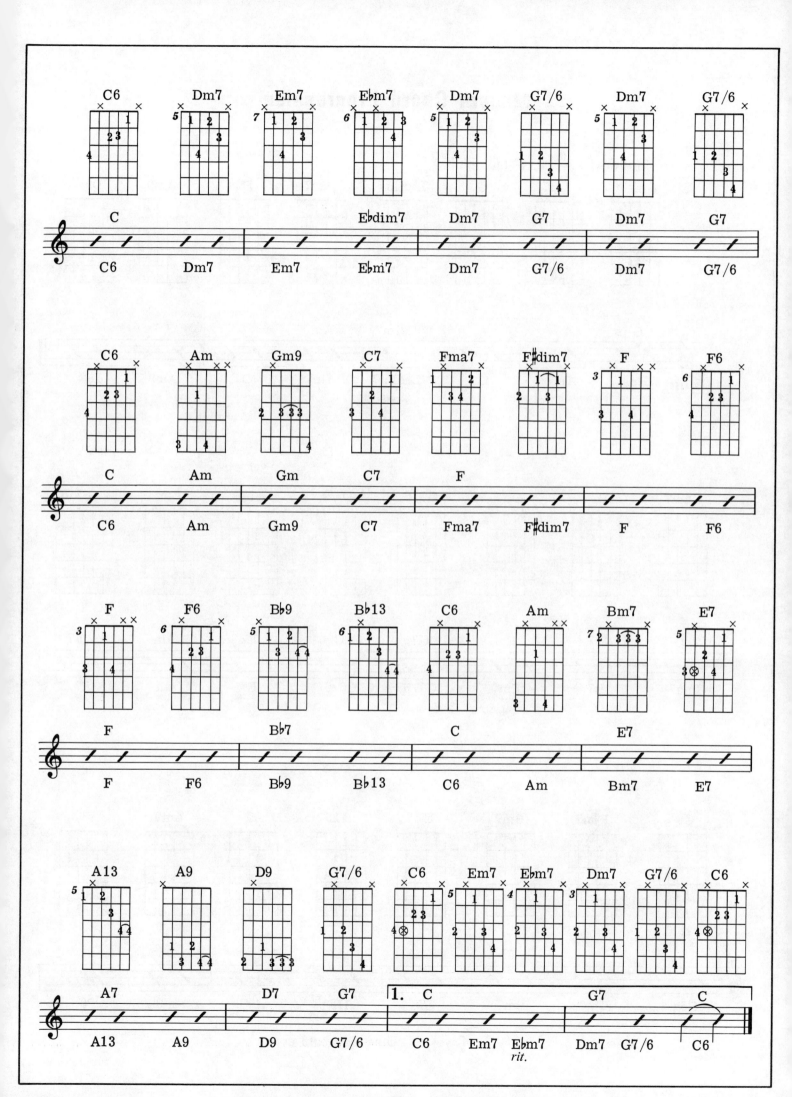

Modern Chord Progression

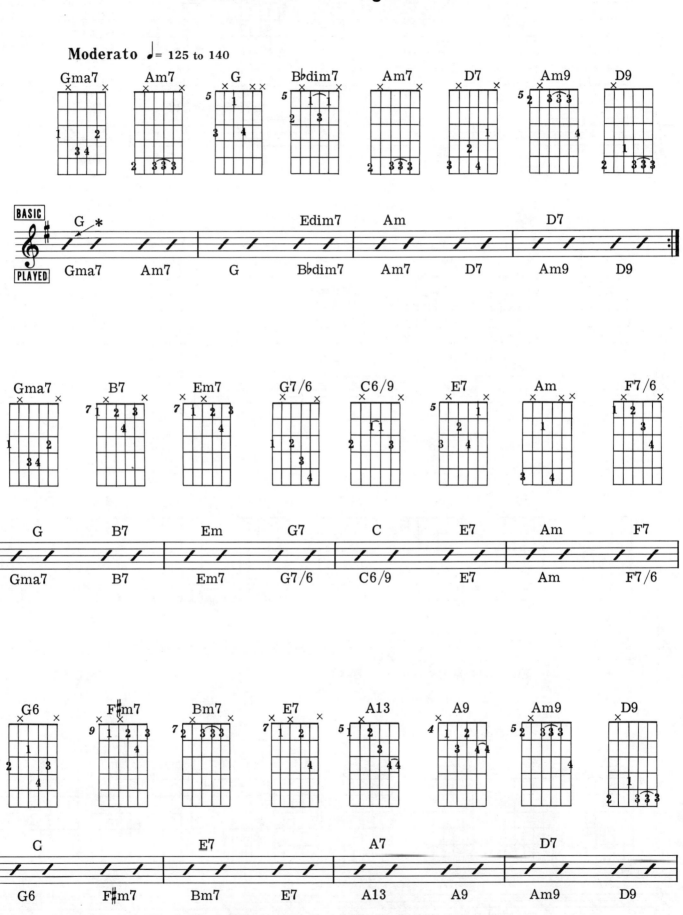

Moderato ♩ = 125 to 140

* Also play | ♩ ♪ ♪ ♩ ♪ ♪ | where applicable.

56

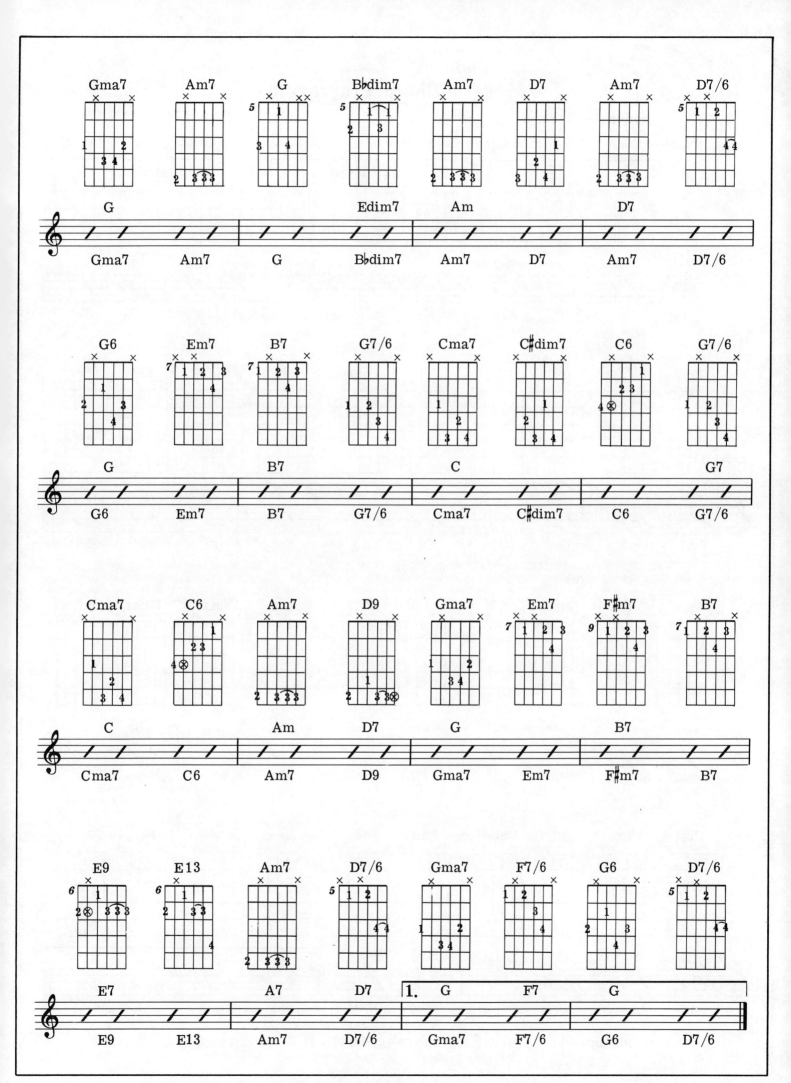

Modern Chord Progression

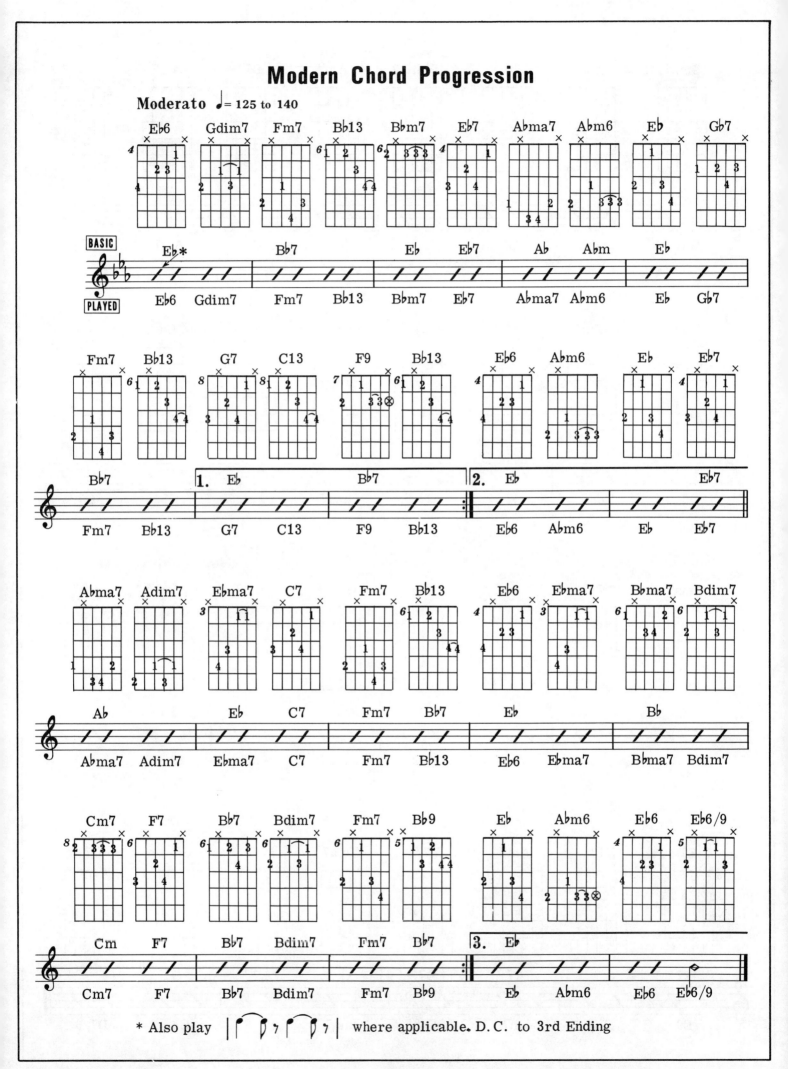

* Also play | ♪ ♪ ♪ ♪ | where applicable. D.C. to 3rd Ending

58

Part—2
Dominant 7th Substitute Chords

The dominant 7th substitute chord is most frequently used to take the place of the original dominant 7th chord (V7). The substitute chord letter name is the flat 5th (b5) of the original V7 chord. For example: The substitute chord for C7, is Gb7; the subst. chord for D7, is Ab7; the subst. chord for Bb7., is E7; the subst. chord for G7, is Db7; etc. Usually the substitute chord sounds better as a 9th, aug. 11th, or 13th chord.

Memorize and master thoroughly each chord progression example in the same procedure as before, and move up one fret chromatically each time to new key and apply the same formations and progression as in the original. Continue thru the key of G.

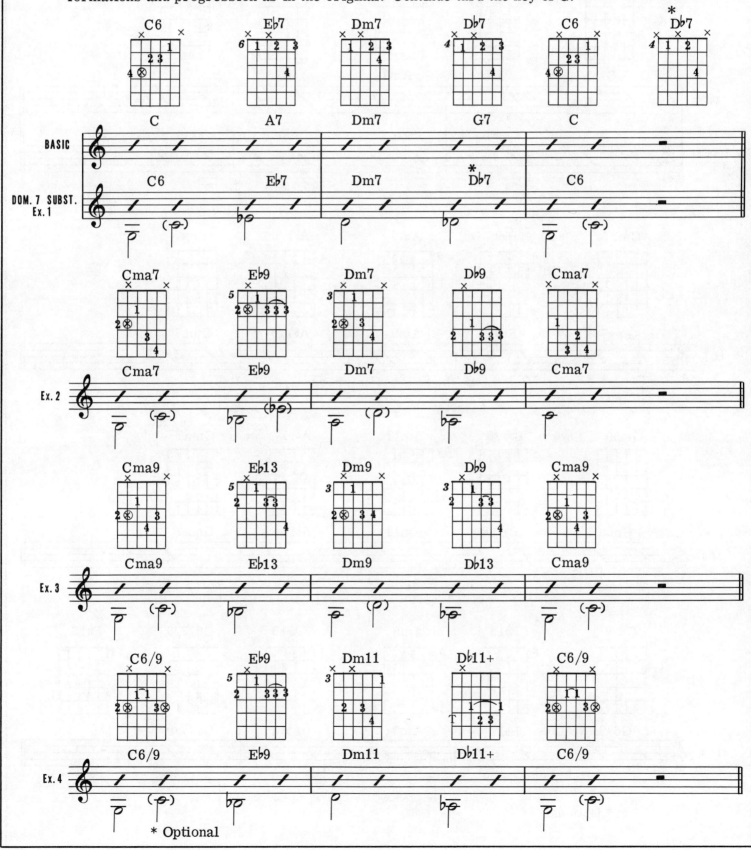

* Optional

59

Familiarize yourself thoroughly with all new chords in charts before attempting to play any of the examples in exercise below. Chords given are of the most popular ones.

Memorize and master thoroughly each chord progression example in the same procedure as before, and move up one fret chromatically each time to new key and apply the same formations and progression as in the original. Continue thru the key of C.

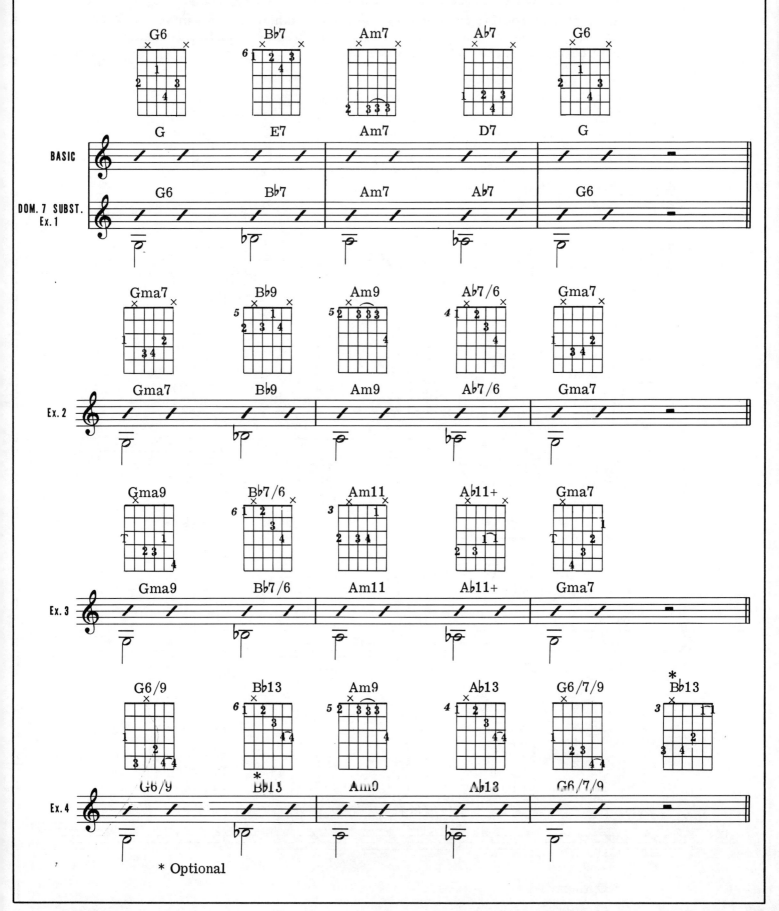

* Optional

Familiarize yourself thoroughly with all new chords in charts before attempting to play any of the examples in exercise below.   Chords given are of the most popular ones.

Memorize and master thoroughly each chord progression example in the same procedure as before, moving up one fret chromatically each time to new key, etc.

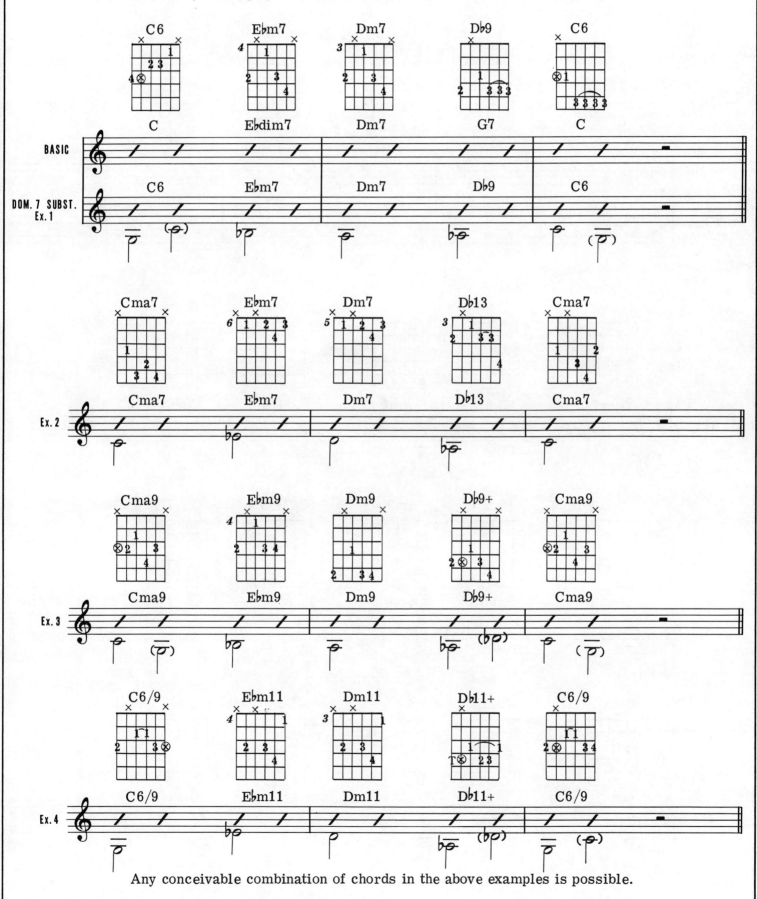

Any conceivable combination of chords in the above examples is possible.

Familiarize yourself thoroughly with all new chords in charts before attempting to play any of the examples in exercise below. Chords given are of the most popular ones.

Memorize and master thoroughly each chord progression example in the same procedure as before, moving up one fret chromatically each time to new key, etc.

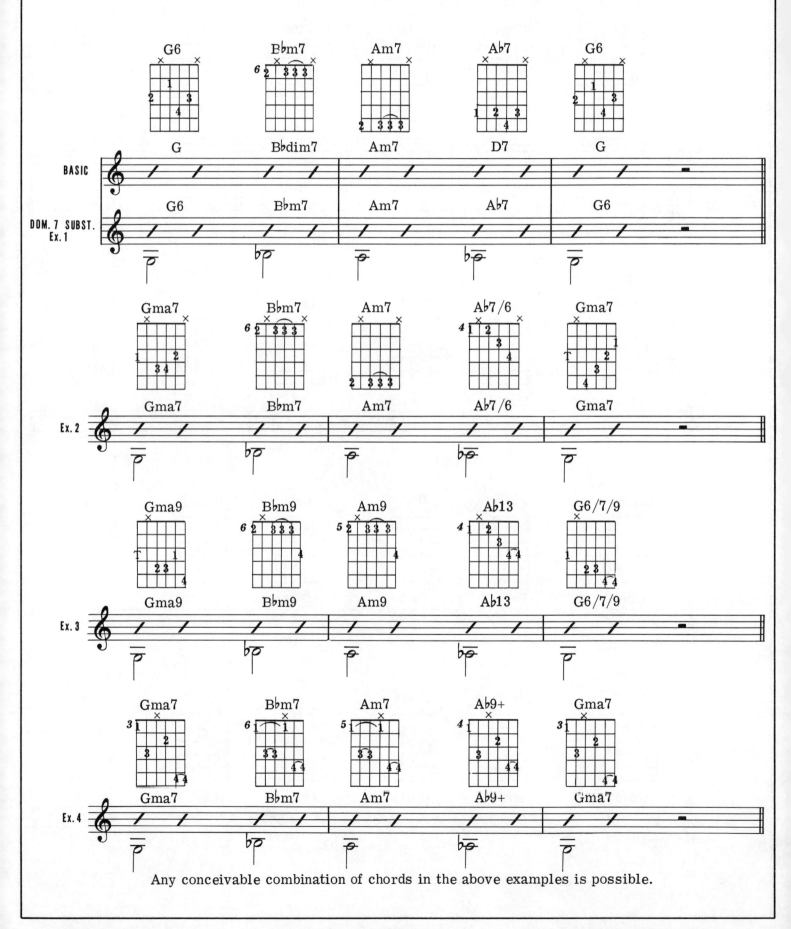

Any conceivable combination of chords in the above examples is possible.

Familiarize yourself thoroughly with all new chords in charts before attempting to play any of the examples in exercise below. Chords given are of the most popular ones.

Memorize and master thoroughly each chord progression example in the same procedure as before, and move up one fret chromatically each time to new key applying the same formations and progression as in original.

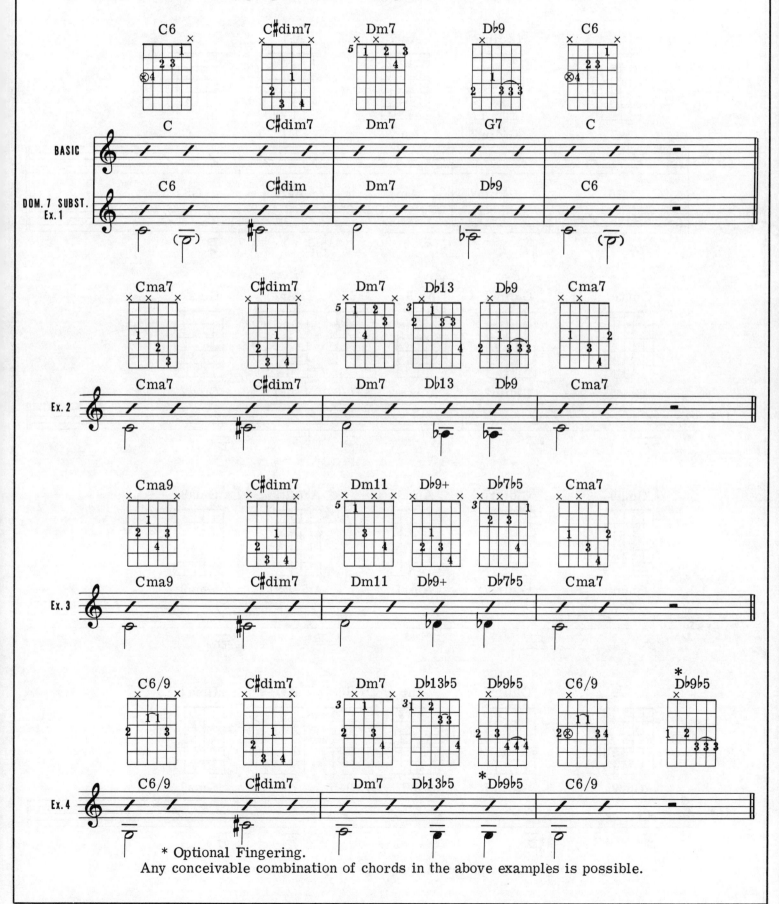

* Optional Fingering.

Any conceivable combination of chords in the above examples is possible.

Familiarize yourself thoroughly with all new chords in charts before attempting to play any of the examples in exercise below. Chords given are of the most popular ones.

Memorize and master thoroughly each chord progression example in the same procedure as before, and move up one fret chromatically each time to new key applying the same formations and progression as in original.

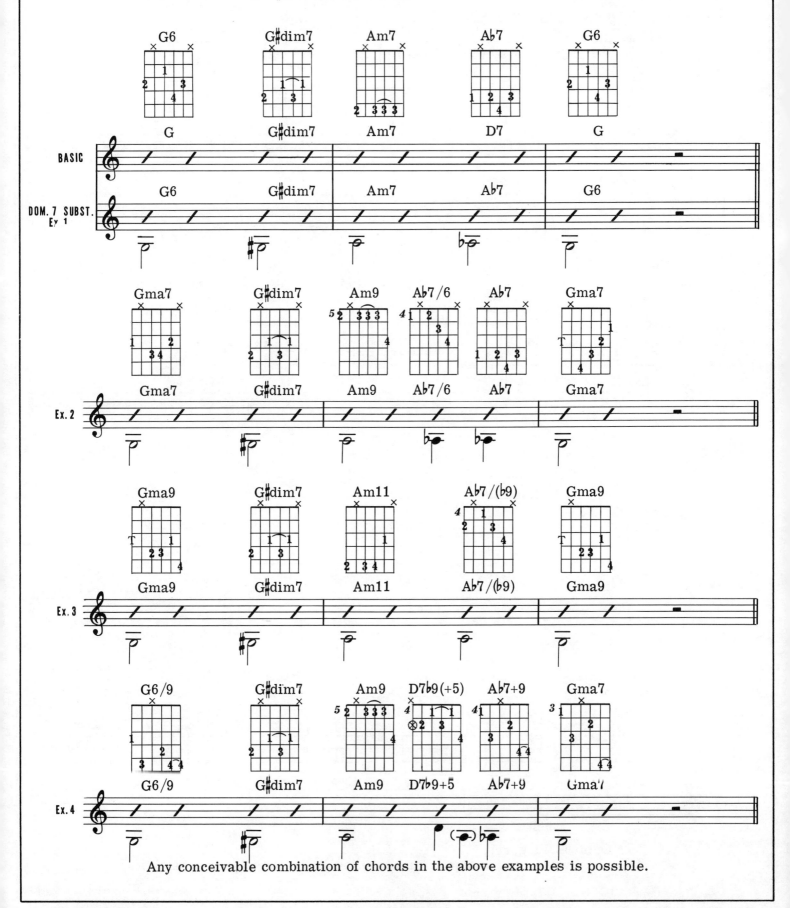

Any conceivable combination of chords in the above examples is possible.

II7 to V7 Substitute Chords

The II7 to V7 substitute chord progression is the same as in a previous exercise with the exception that the original V7 chord is substituted with another dominant - type chord. (See Dominant 7th substitute chords.) Familiarize yourself thoroughly with all II7 to V7 substitute chord progressions in all keys. These chords may be extended as previously.

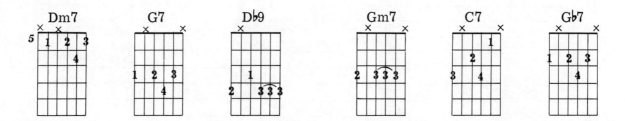

Memorize and master thoroughly each chord progression example in the same proce-dure as before, and move up one fret chromatically each time to new key applying the same formations and progression as in original.

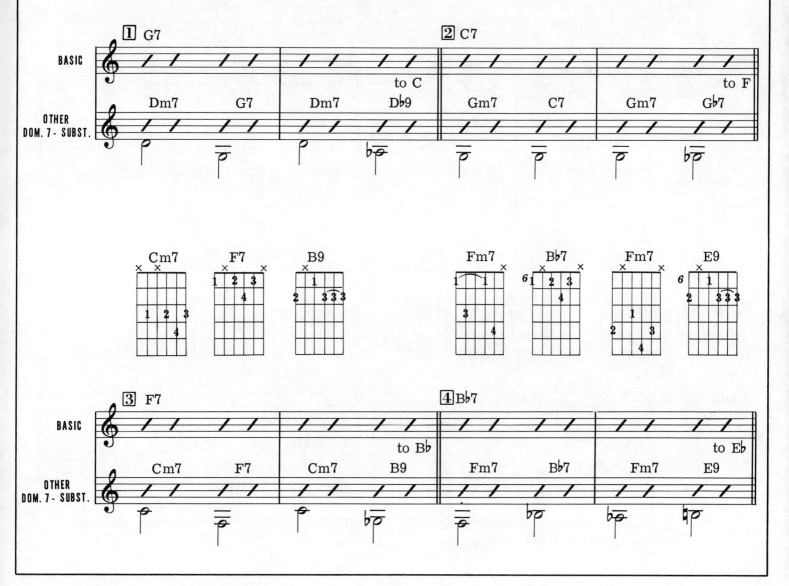

Minor 6th Substitute Chords

The minor 6th substitute chord is a dominant 9th (aug. 11th or 13th) chord. To determine the letter name for the minor 6th substitute chord, several rules may be used; however, the one most accepted is the one whose letter name is a 5th below that of the original minor 6th chord. For example: The subst. chord for Cm6, is F9; for Gm6, is C9; for Dm6, is G9, etc.

MINOR 6TH	SUBSTITUTE CHORD	MINOR 6TH	SUBSTITUTE CHORD
Gm6	C9	Cm6	F9
Dm6	G9	Fm6	Bb9
Am6	D9	Bbm6	Eb9
Em6	A9	Ebm6	Ab9
Bm6	E9	Abm6	Db9
F#m6	B9	Dbm6	Gb9
C#m6	F#9	Gbm6	Cb9
G#m6	C#9		

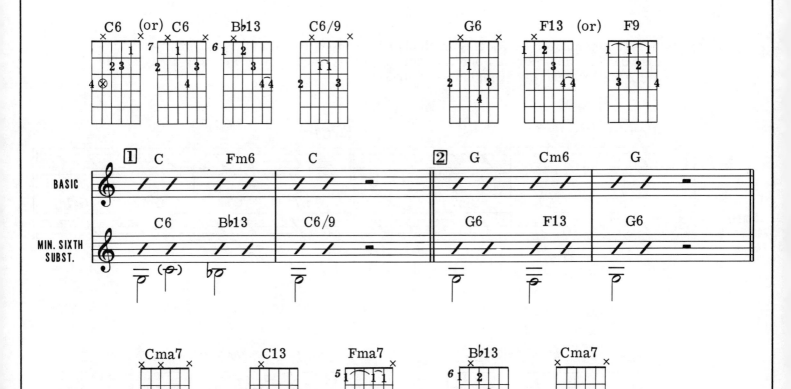

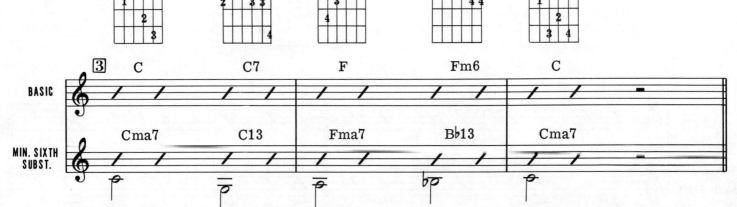

Familiarize yourself thoroughly with all minor 6th substitute chords in all keys, using the examples given as a guide.

Fill–in Progressions–Dom. 7th Subst. Chords

Fill - in progressions with dominant 7th substitute chords, sometimes called a turn-around in a song, are very effective and frequently used. A fill - in, turn - around progression, may be used at the end of the first 8 measure phrase, and at the conclusion of a song when the chorus is repeated. However, fill - in, turn - around progressions may also be used for introductions and endings. Note the chords in the basic progression and the choice of chords used for fill - in and substitute chords. Play these in different keys.

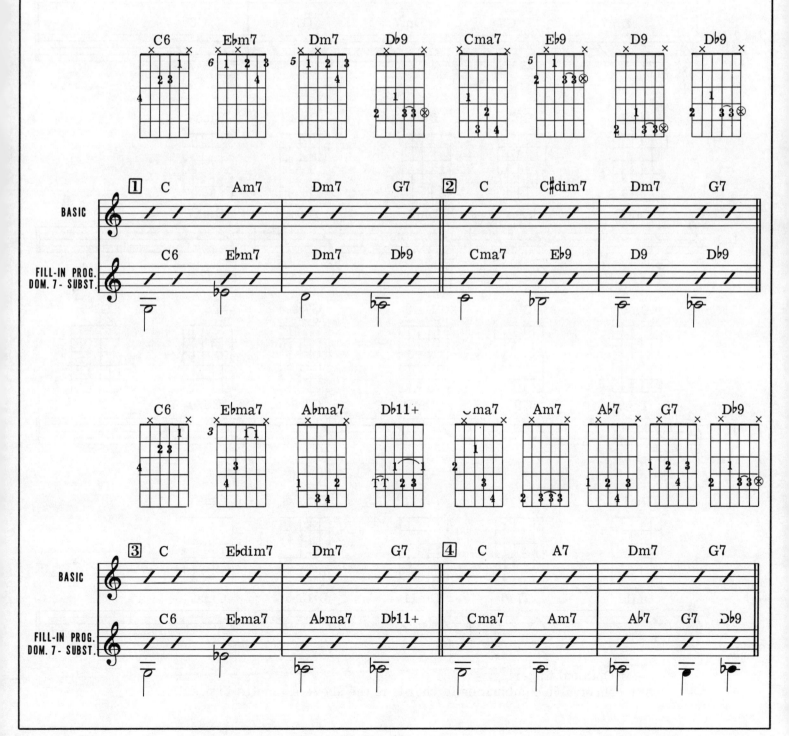

Altered Dom. 7th – Substitute Chords

A thorough study of altered dominant 7th and dominant 7th substitute chords is essential. However, other altered dominant 7th and dominant substitute chords should be utilized besides the ones given in the examples. Memorize and master thoroughly each chord progression example as before, moving up one fret chromatically each time to new key, etc. Continue this procedure in other keys.

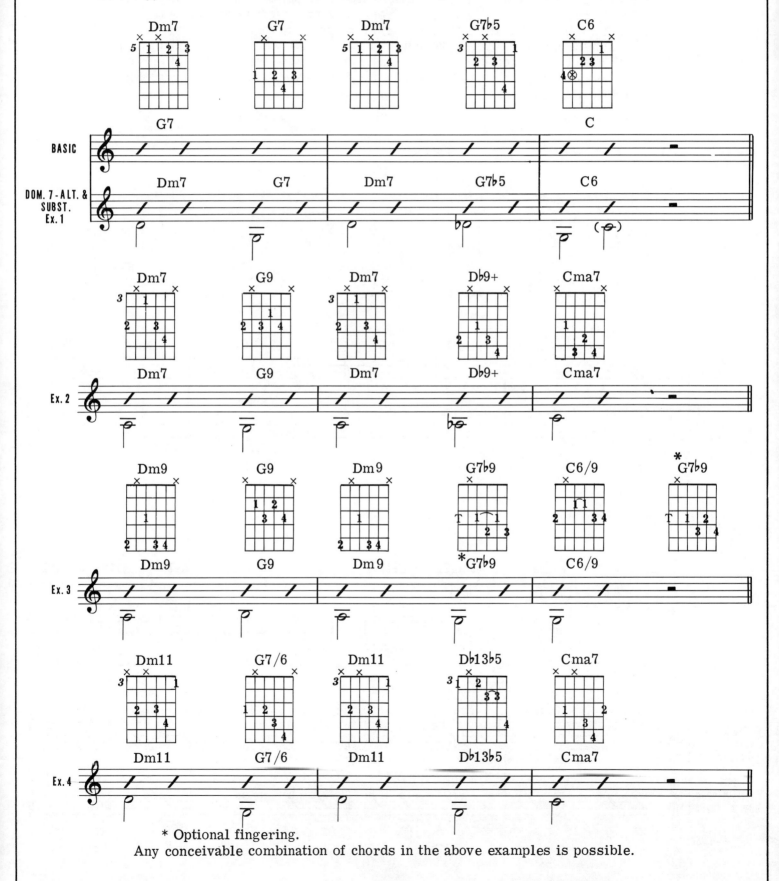

* Optional fingering.
Any conceivable combination of chords in the above examples is possible.

Altered Dom. 7th – Substitute Chords

Memorize and master thoroughly each chord progression example in the same procedure as before, and move up one fret chromatically each time to new key applying the same formations and progression as in original.

Familiarize yourself thoroughly with all new chords in charts before attempting to play any of the examples in exercise below. Chords given are of the most popular ones.

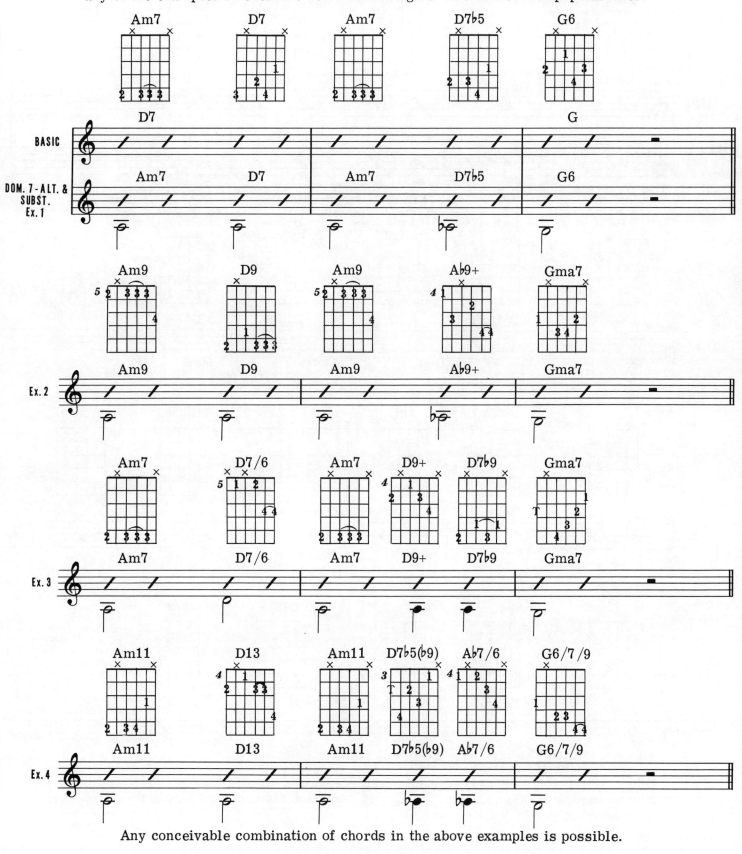

Any conceivable combination of chords in the above examples is possible.

Alt. Dom. & Subst. Chords

Memorize and master thoroughly each chord progression example in the same procedure as before, and move DOWN one fret chromatically each time to new key applying the same formations and progression as in original. Continue downward thru the key of Db.

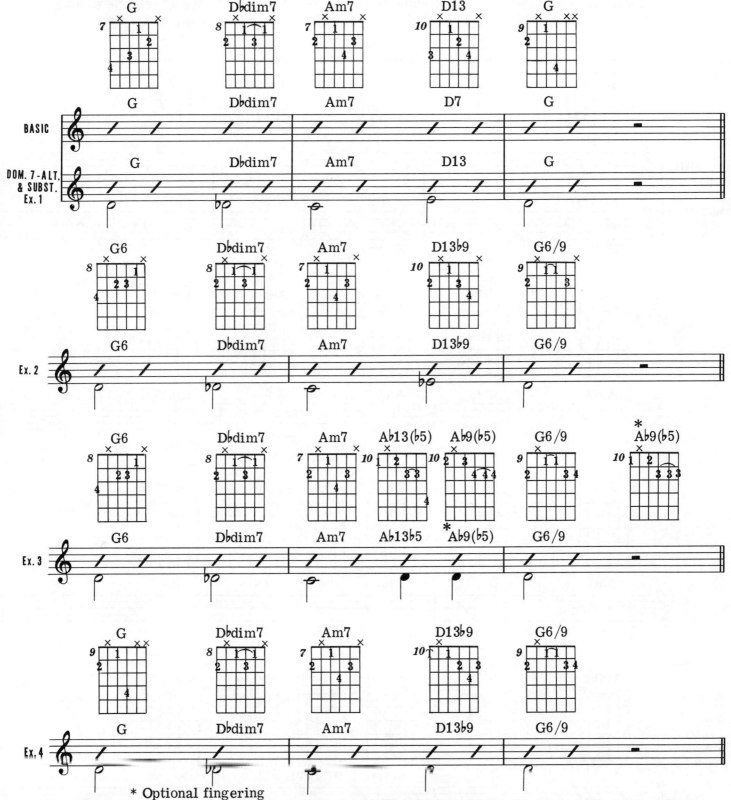

* Optional fingering

Other altered dominant and dominant substitute chords besides the ones given in examples may be used. For other selection of altered dominant chord dominant substitute chords-see the author's CHORD BOOK-

Any conceivable combination of chords in the above examples is possible.

III Chord – Alt. Dom. & Substitute

Memorize and master thoroughly each chord progression example in the same procedure as before, and move up one fret chromatically each time to new key applying the same formations and progression as in original. Continue thru the key of F.

Familiarize yourself thoroughly with all new chords in charts before attempting to play any of the examples in exercise below. Chords given are of the most popular ones.

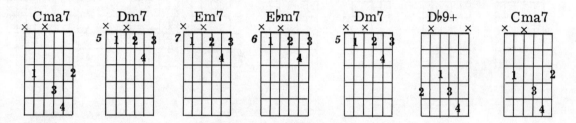

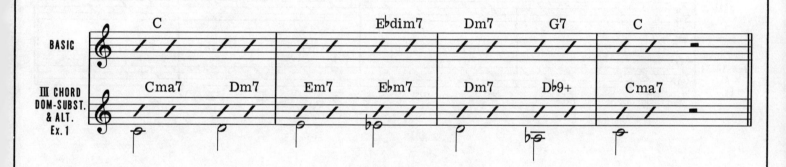

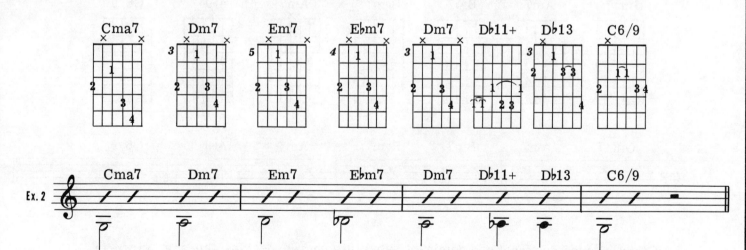

Other altered dominant substitute chords besides the ones given in examples may be used; such as Db7b5; Db7+5; Db7b9; Db13b9, etc. Continue this procedure in other keys. For other selection of dominant substitute and altered chords–see the author's CHORD BOOK–

Proceed as before with other extensions for Major, Minor, and Dominant type chords not given in the above examples. Any conceivable combination of chords in the above examples is possible.

Memorize and master thoroughly each chord progression example in the same procedure as before, and move up one fret chromatically each time to new key applying the same formations and progression as in original. Continue thru the key of C.

Familiarize yourself thoroughly with all new chords in charts before attempting to play any of the examples in exercise below. Chords given are of the most popular ones.

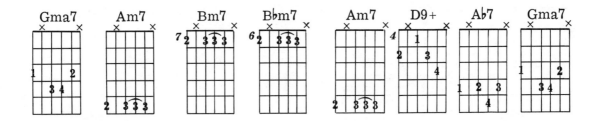

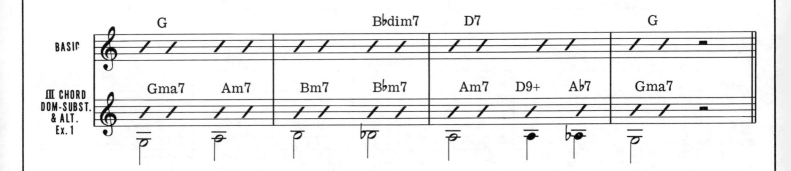

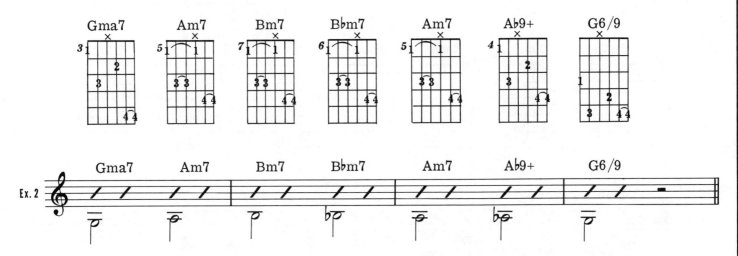

Other altered dominant and dominant substitute chords besides the ones given in example may be used; such as - D7b9; D7b5; D13b9, etc. Altered dominant substitute chords; such as - Ab7+5; Ab13b9; Ab7b9; Ab11+, etc. Use good taste in selecting the proper chords. See author's CHORD BOOK for selection of other altered dominant and substitute chords.

Proceed as before with other extensions for Major, Minor, and Dominant type chords not given in the above examples. Any conceivable combination of chords in the above examples is possible.

Alt. Dom. 7th - Subst. Chords

Memorize and master thoroughly each chord progression example in the same procedure as before, moving up one fret chromatically each time applying same formation, etc. Play each progression in several keys.

Familiarize yourself thoroughly with all new chords in charts before attempting to play any of the examples in exercise below. Chords given are of the most popular ones.

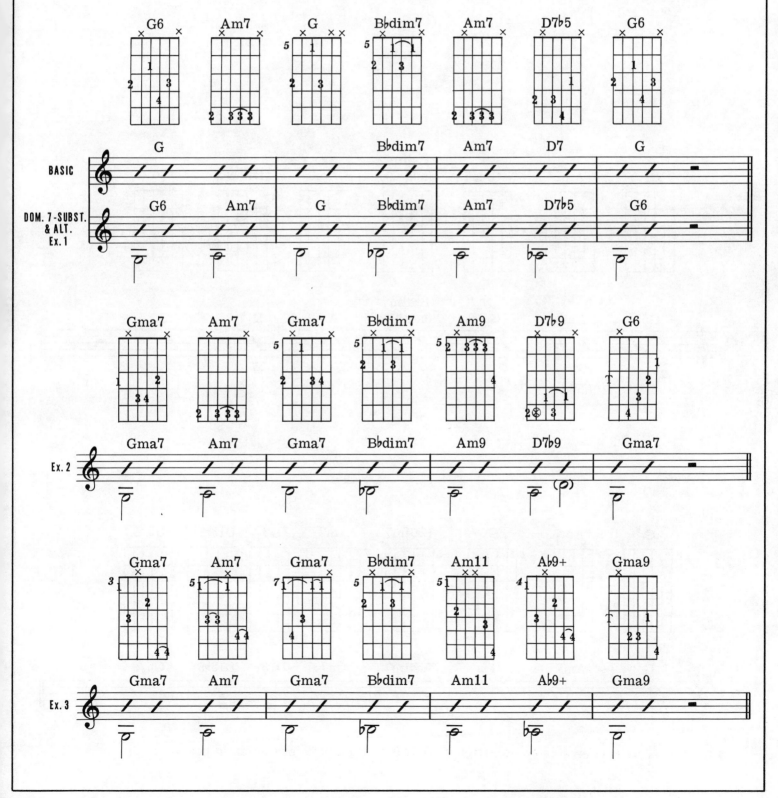

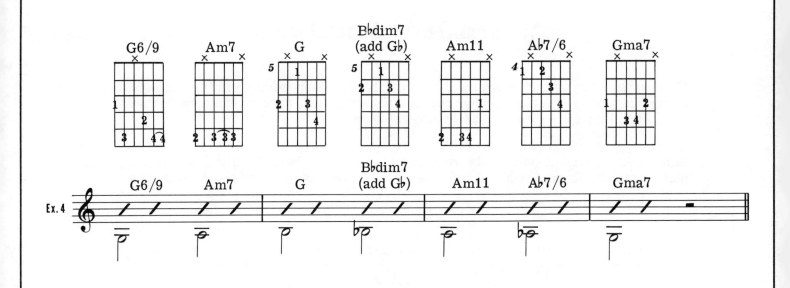

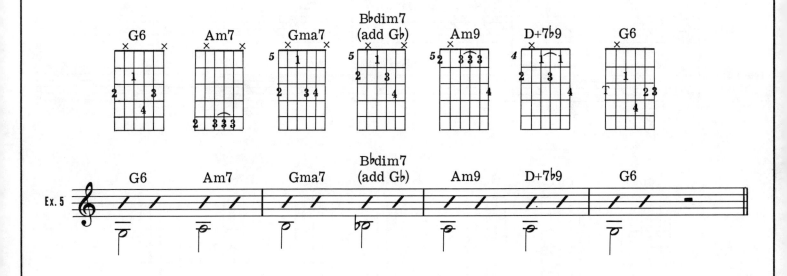

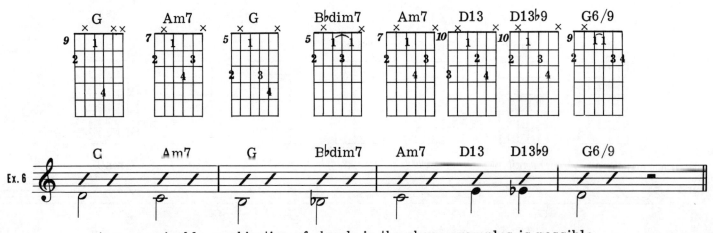

Any conceivable combination of chords in the above examples is possible.

Alt. Dom. & Subst. Chords

In the three (3) examples given below, memorize and master each progression before moving up one fret chromatically each time to new key and applying the same formations and progression as in original. Continue each example thru the key of G.

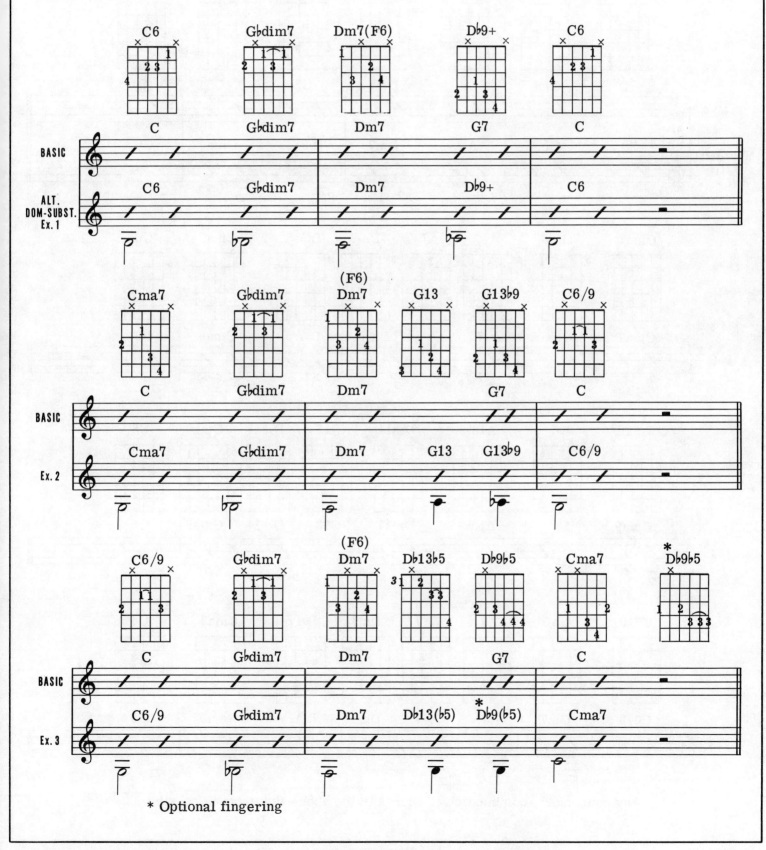

* Optional fingering

Alt. Dom. 7th & Subst. Chords

Memorize and master thoroughly each chord progression example in the same procedure as before, and move up one fret chromatically each time to new key applying the same formations and progression as in original. Continue thru the key of G.

Familiarize yourself thoroughly with all new chords in charts before attempting to play any of the examples in exercise below. Chords given are of the most popular ones.

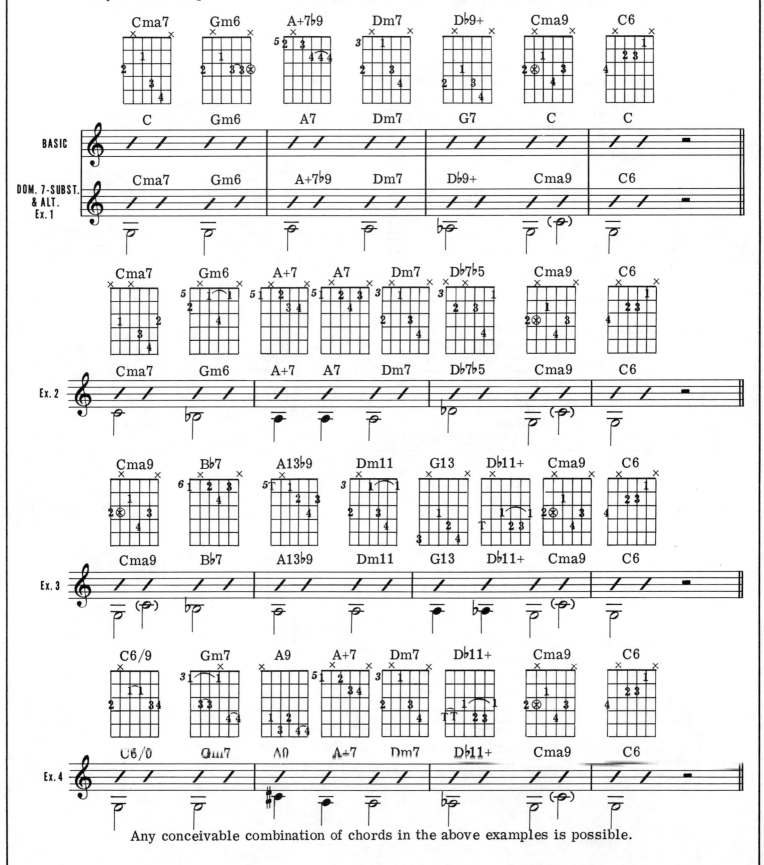

Any conceivable combination of chords in the above examples is possible.

Chrom. Prog. Alt. Dom. 7th & Subst. Chords

Memorize and master thoroughly each chord progression example in the same procedure as before, moving up one fret chromatically each time applying same formations, etc. Play each progression in several keys.

Familiarize yourself thoroughly with all new chords in charts before attempting to play any of the examples in exercise below. Chords given are of the most popular ones.

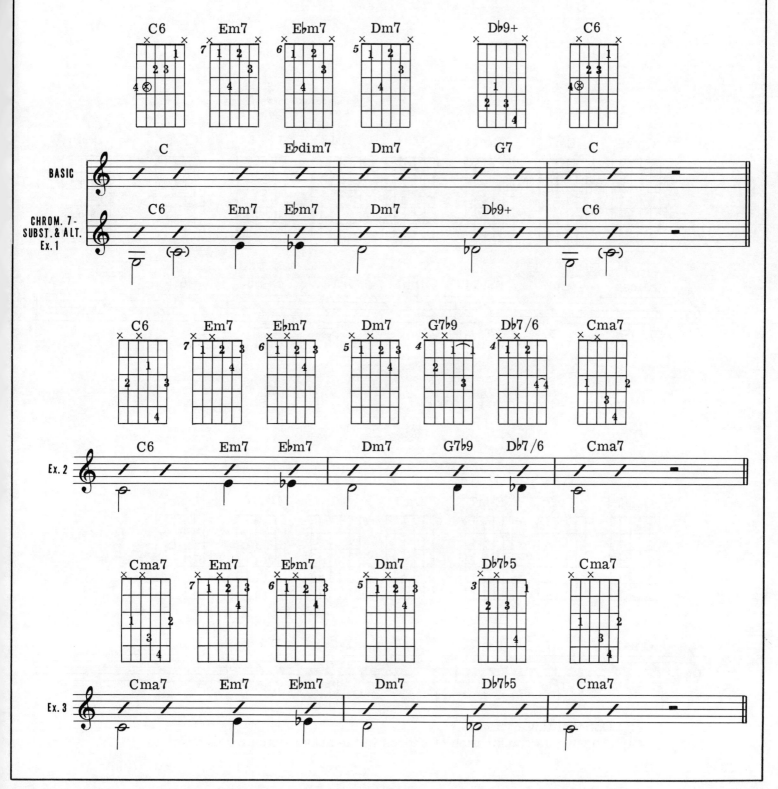

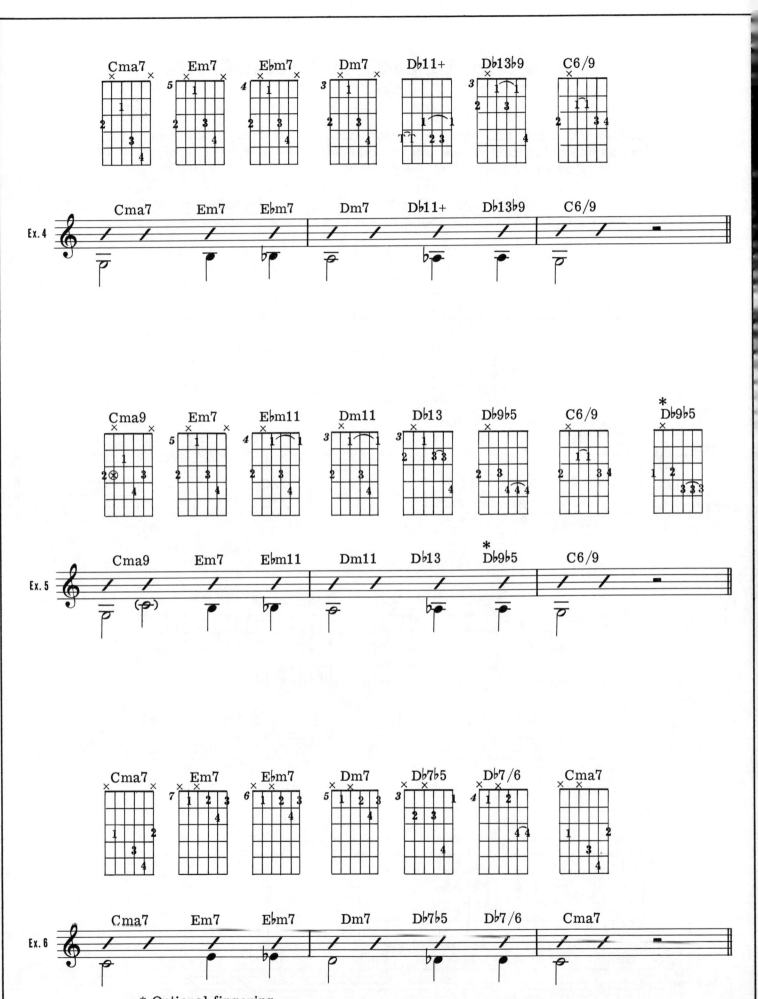

* Optional fingering
Any conceivable combination of chords in the above examples is possible.

Fill - in Chords - Alt. Dom. 7th & Subst.

Memorize and master thoroughly each chord progression example in the same procedure as before, moving up one fret chromatically each time applying same formation, etc. Play each progression in several keys.

Familiarize yourself thoroughly with all new chords in charts before attempting to play any of the examples in exercise below. Chords given are of the most popular ones.

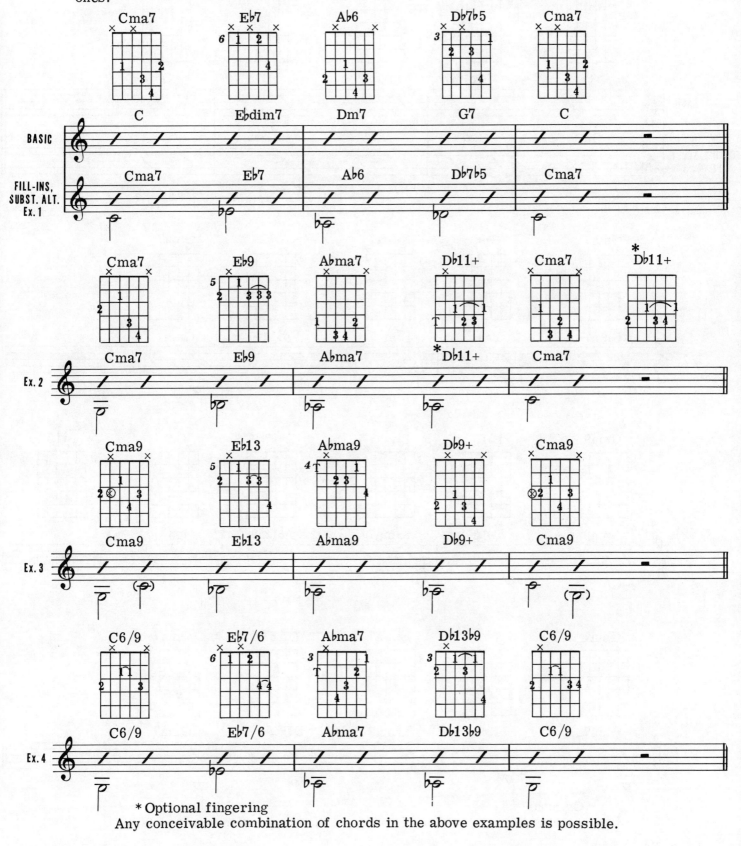

*Optional fingering
Any conceivable combination of chords in the above examples is possible.

Memorize and master thoroughly each chord progression example in the same procedure as before, moving up one fret chromatically each time applying same formation, etc. Play each progression in several keys.

Familiarize yourself thoroughly with all new chords in charts before attempting to play any of the examples in exercise below. Chords given are of the most popular ones.

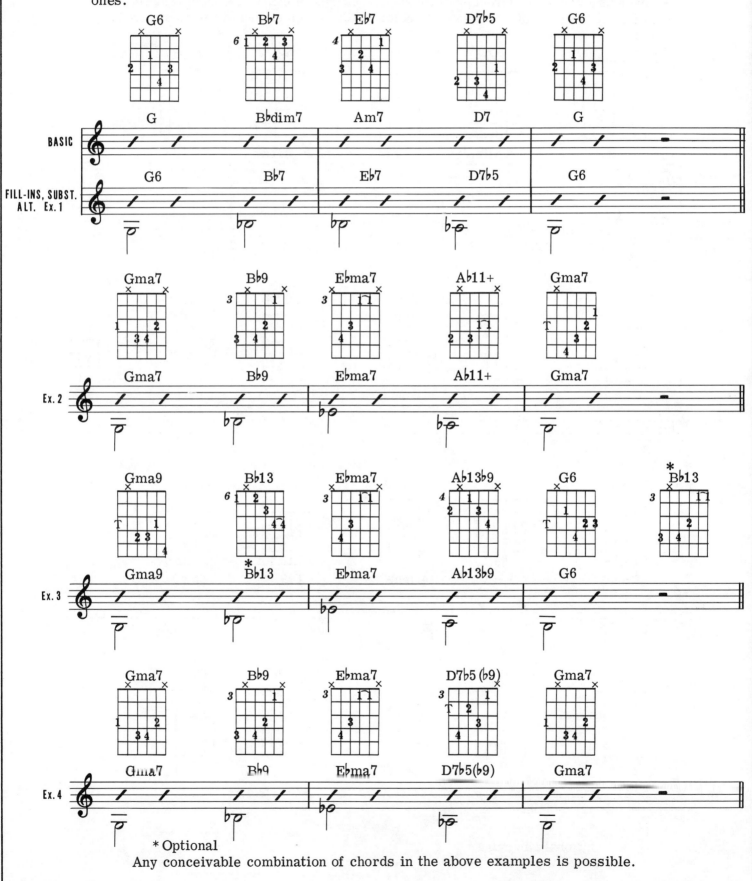

*Optional

Any conceivable combination of chords in the above examples is possible.

Chrom. Prog. - Alt. Dom. 7th & Subst. Chords

Memorize and master thoroughly each chord progression example in the same procedure as before, moving up one fret chromatically each time, applying same formation, etc. Play each progression in several keys.

Familiarize yourself thoroughly with all new chords in charts before attempting to play any of the examples in exercise below. Chords given are of the most popular ones.

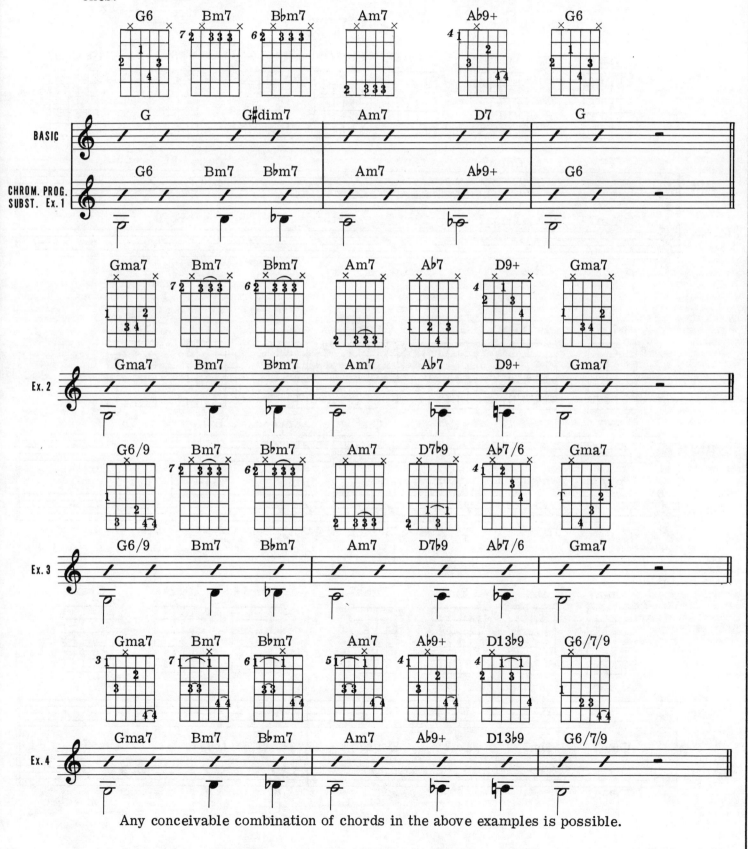

Any conceivable combination of chords in the above examples is possible.

Other Fill - in, Subst. & Alt. Chords

In the examples to follow, these chord progressions can be used as Fill-ins, Endings, Introductions, Substitutions, etc. Familiarize yourself thoroughly with each example and play each in several keys.

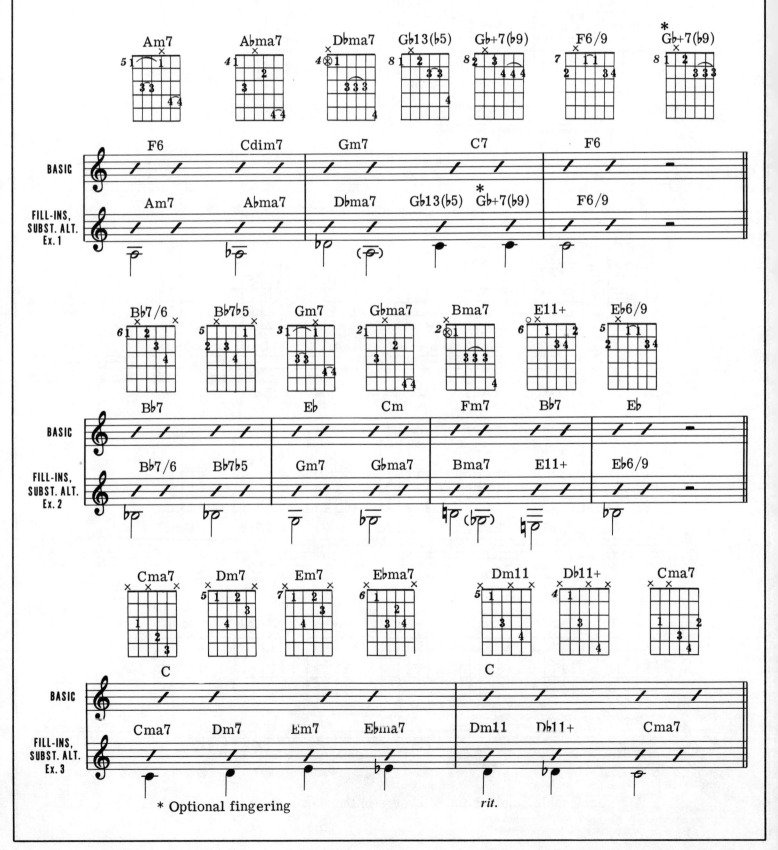

* Optional fingering

rit.

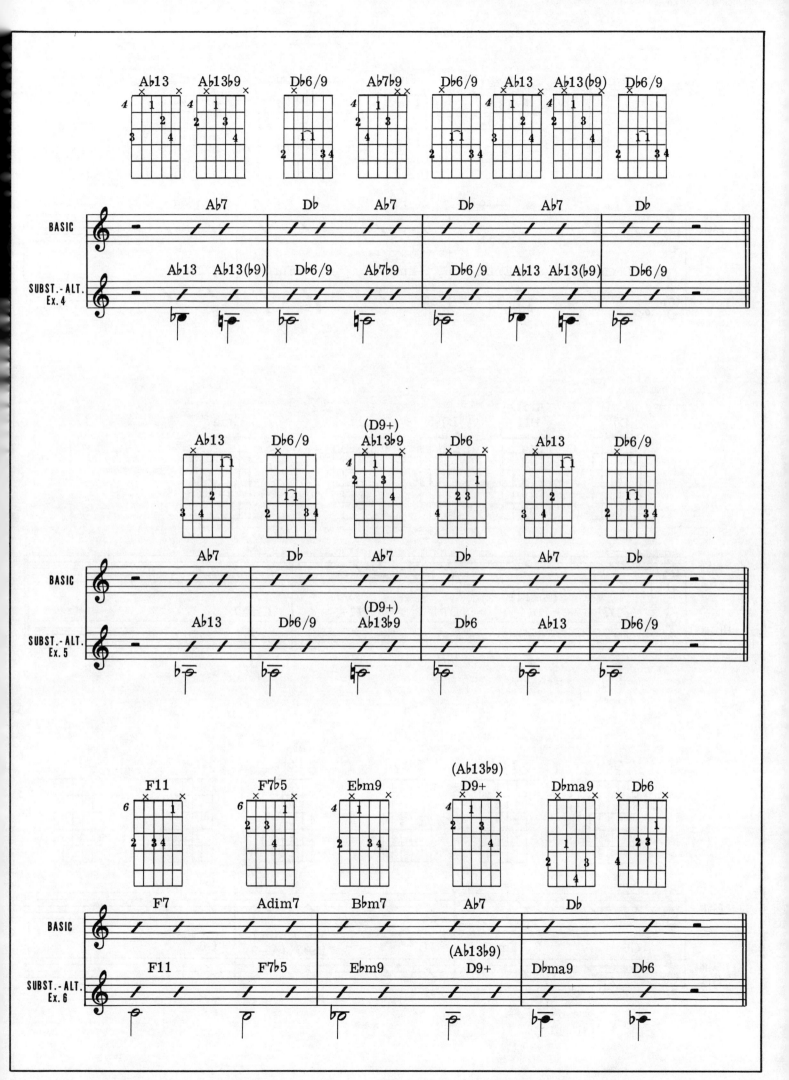

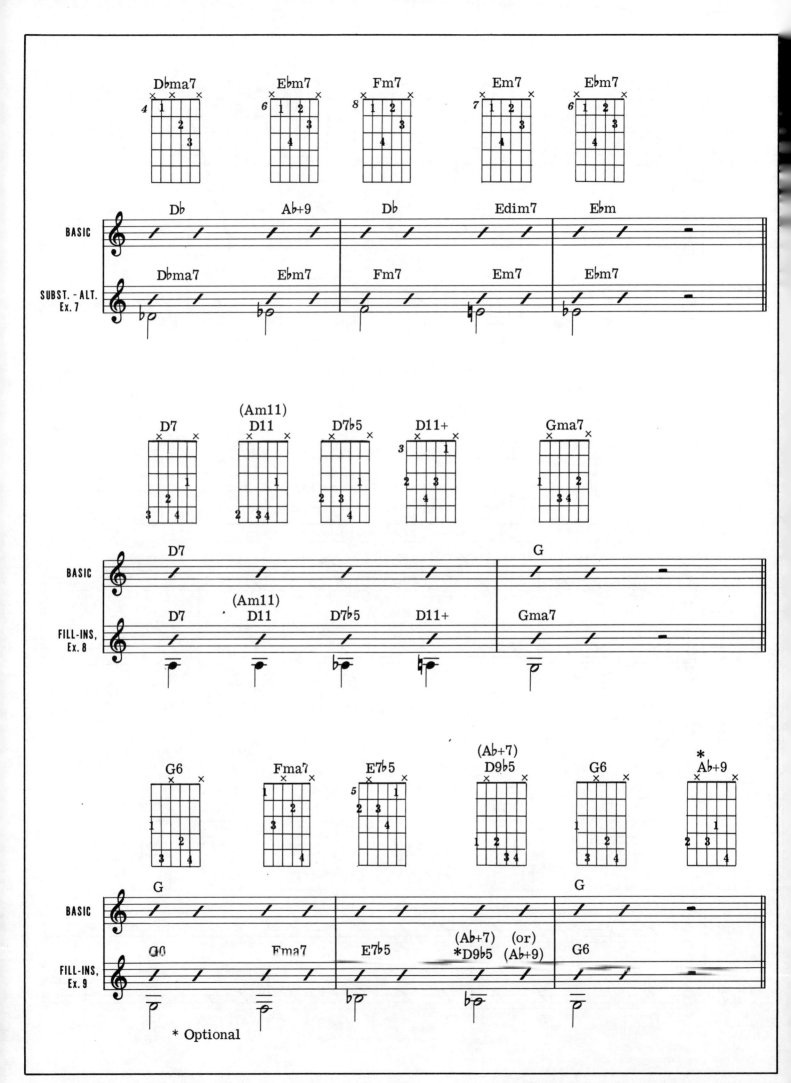

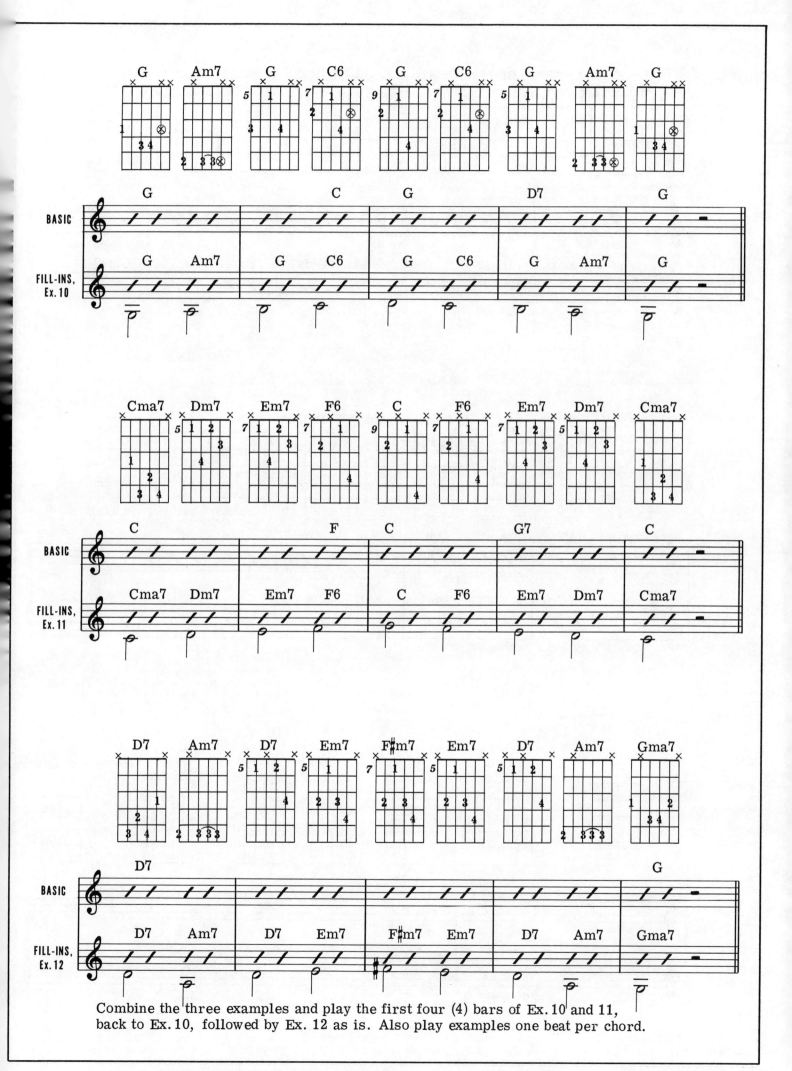

Combine the three examples and play the first four (4) bars of Ex. 10 and 11, back to Ex. 10, followed by Ex. 12 as is. Also play examples one beat per chord.

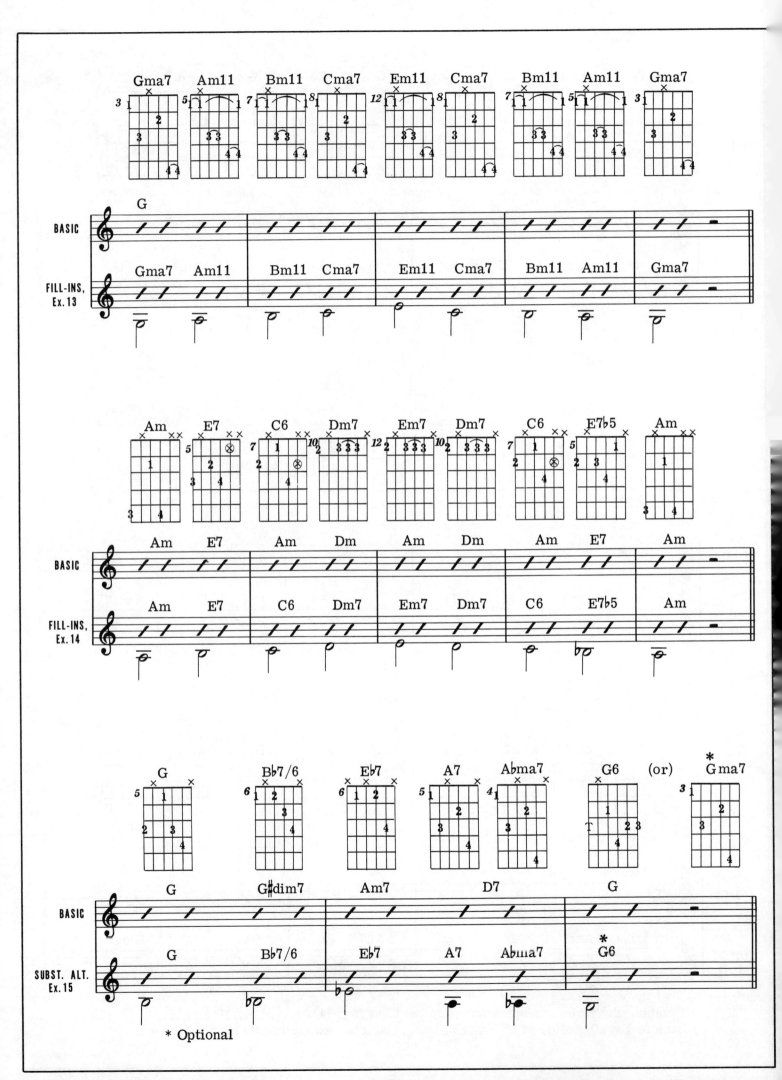

Turn - Arounds/Endings

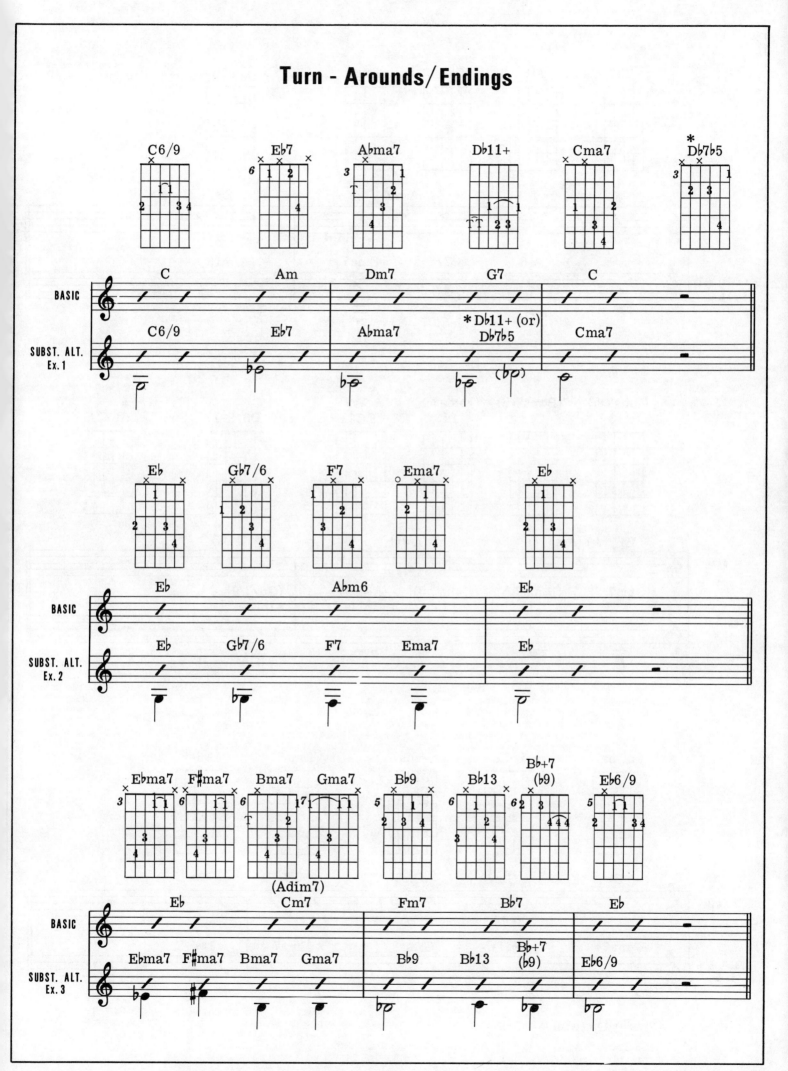

87

Modern Chord Progression

Familiarize yourself thoroughly with all chords in charts before attempting to play the chord progression below. Chords given are of the most popular ones.

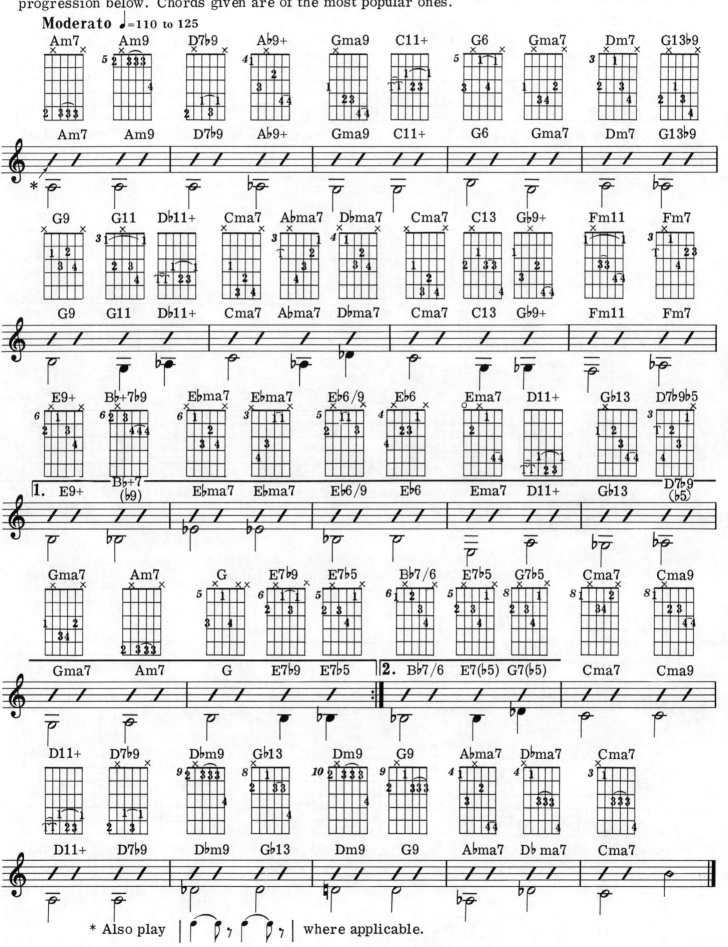

Modern Chord Progression

Familiarize yourself thoroughly with all chords in charts before attempting to play the chord progression below. Chords given are of the most popular ones.

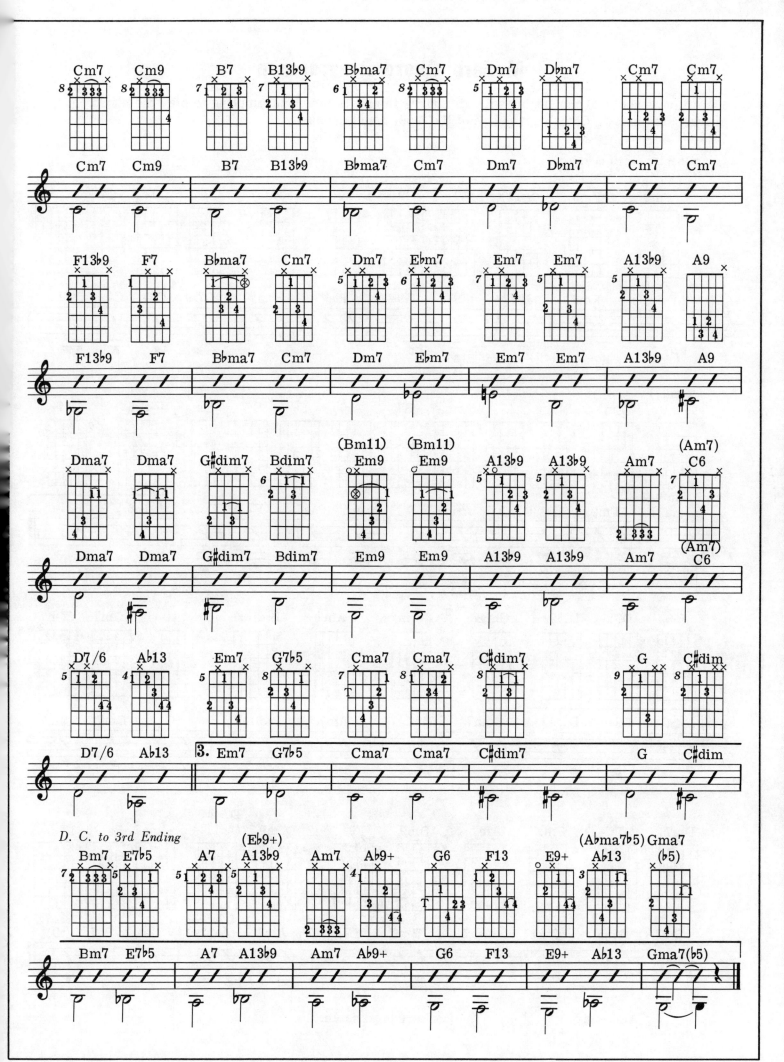

Modern Chord Progression

Familiarize yourself thoroughly with all chords in charts before attempting to play the chord progression below. Chords given are of the most popular ones.

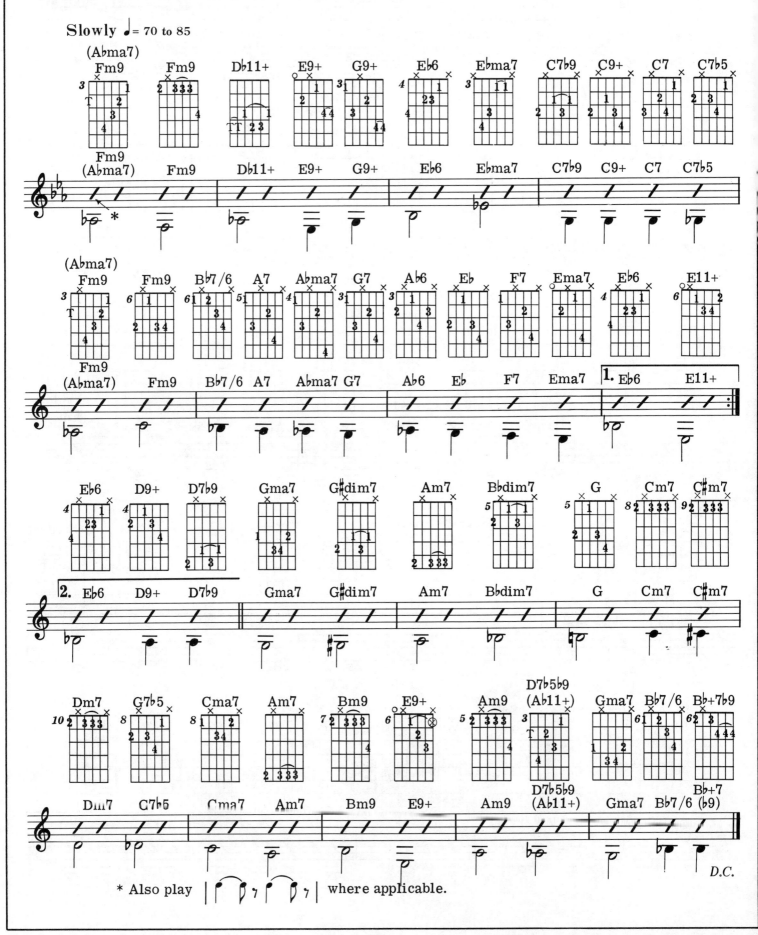

* Also play where applicable.

Modern Chord Progression

The Modern Chord Progressions to follow consist of extensions, alterations, and substitutions utilizing some of the possibilities that may be achieved. However, the examples given do not indicate the ultimate that can be achieved thru proper utilization and application.

Familiarize yourself thoroughly with all chords in charts before attempting to play the chord progression below. Chords given are of the most popular ones.

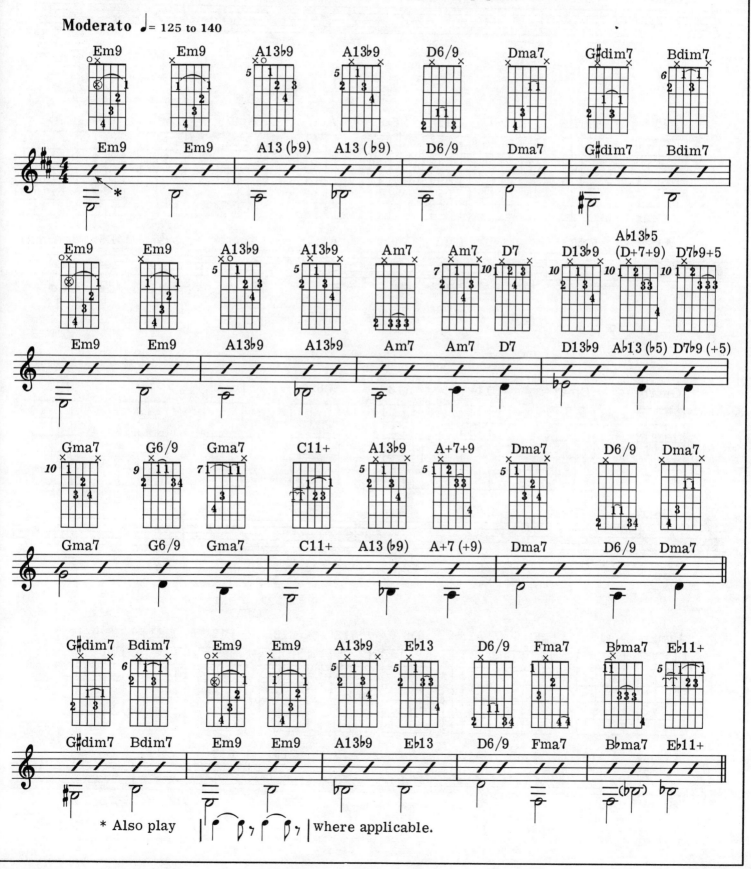

* Also play [rhythm notation] where applicable.

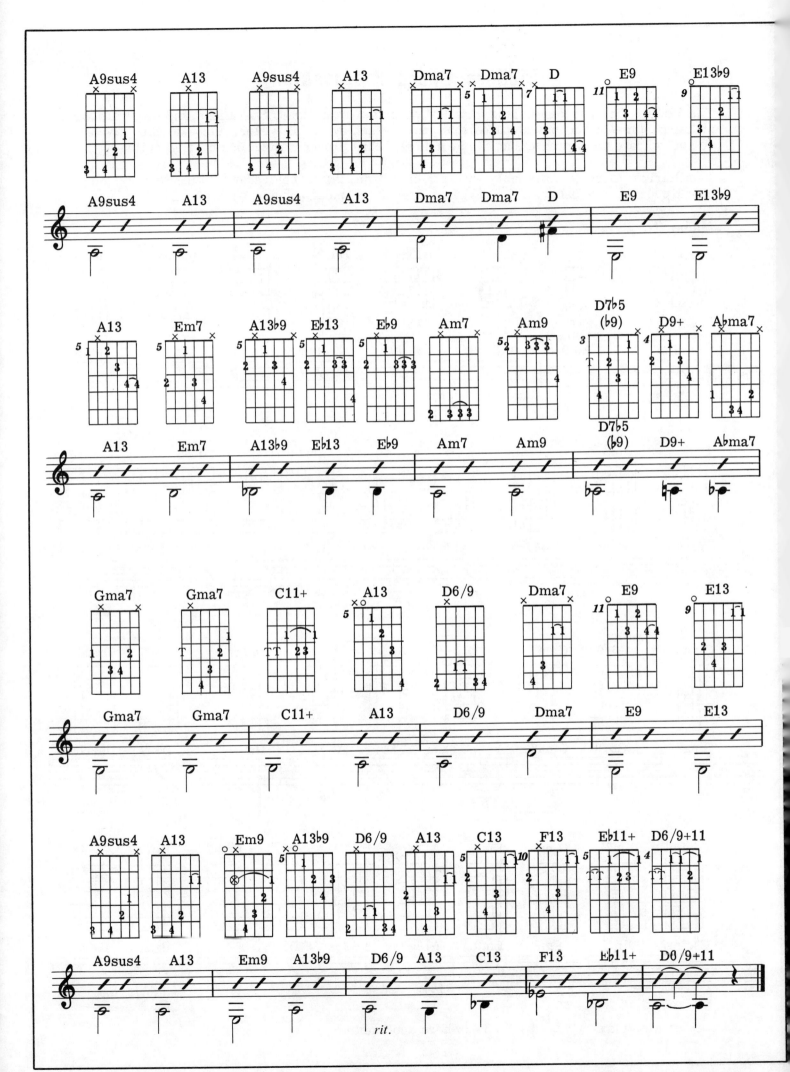

Modern Chord Progression

Familiarize yourself thoroughly with all chords in charts before attempting to play the chord progression below. Chords given are of the most popular ones.

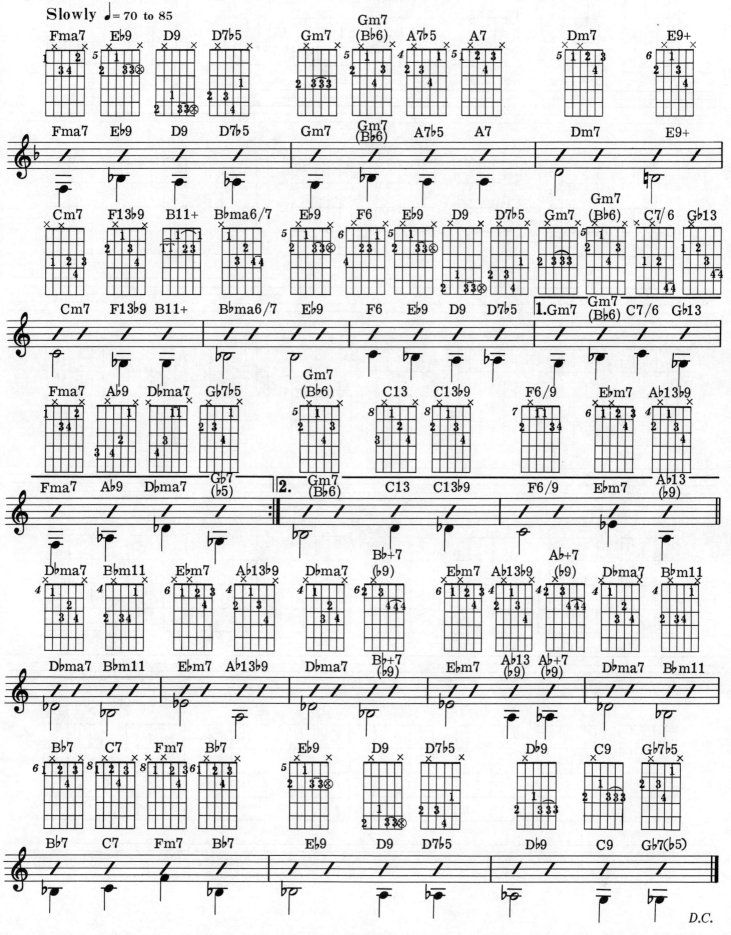

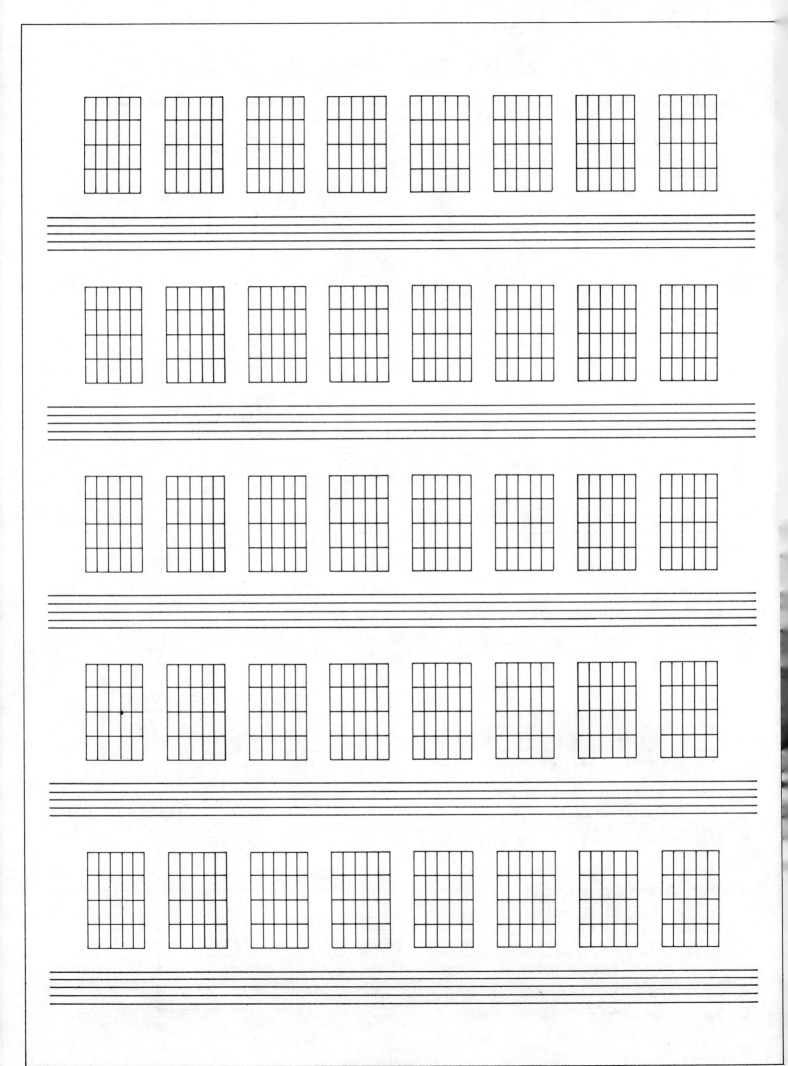